Green Pastures, Still Waters:
Overcoming in The Eye of the Storm
Written by Aurora A. Ambrose

Dedication

To the love of my life, my parents, family and friends, with utmost gratitude for your loving encouragement: Also, to those who have shed light, wisdom and help when I needed it most. Thank you so much for your loving care, prayers, patience, time, support and inspiration.

http://theauroralighthouse.com/

My Purpose: Always Live Sunny Side Up!

O Lord, You are my God; I will exalt You, I will praise Your Name, for You have done wonderful things, even purposes planned of old [and fulfilled] in faithfulness and truth.
- Isaiah 25:1

But for this very purpose have I let you live, that I might show you My Power, and that My Name may be declared throughout all the earth. - Exodus 9:16

All Bible Scriptures are referenced from the King James Version, the New International Version or the Amplified Bible Version, unless otherwise noted.

Table of Contents

My Purpose

Prologue of Purpose: Be Wiser, Rise Higher; Choose Your Attitude and Altitude 1

In Green Pastures, By Still Waters 5

Duh, I Don't Get It 15

In His Holy Presence 23

Practice His Presence 25

Forgive Yourself 27

Grieve and Rejoice 29

The Audacity to Live 34

Transitions 37

Three Essentials of Life 40

Being Crushed in the Olive Press of Life 44

Deep Waters 46

It's Only Temporary 48

Great Pretender 51

Selah 53

What do you do in the eye of the storm? 55

21 Things to Safeguard 62

Being Dressed for Battle: Armed and Dangerous 65

The Armor of God, Our Spiritual Clothing 66

What are you made of? 82

Triumphantly Overcoming a Crushed Spirit 86

Godly Affirmations 89

The Meaning of the Phrase, Dying to Self 97

Encourage Yourself!..104

Praise God from Whom All Blessings Flow: My Levitical Poetic Doxology 105

Psalm 91 Safety in God's Presence...110

Hallelujah, I'm Free!..114

What Do You Do When God Says No? 116

Be a Victor: Overcome Adversity 123

Be Optimistic 131

The Benefits of Staying On the Sunny Side: Research 137

Be just like an Oyster...142

Be Joyful..148

An Experiment 155

Silence and Stillness are Golden and Other Life Lessons 161

Be a Friend of Change 167

Help and Joy in the Midst of the Storm.....................................169

God's Boxes 173

Be Wise with Your Greatest Power...175

Reflect and Redirect 179

The Best Day Ever 184

Seeing with New Eyes...188

The Bee-Attitudes...191

Life Lessons in the Aloha Wave..193

Epilogue: Let Your Spirit Be Positive 196

About the Author..199

About the Book, ...201

Prologue of Purpose:
Be Wiser, Rise Higher
Choose Your Attitude and Altitude

Truly, one's attitude determines one's altitude in life's journey. That attitude or perspective colors everything in life. In my opinion, the more positive the attitude, the higher the altitude to be achieved. Therefore, your perspective is your elective. That said, living sunny side up, like a fresh daisy, upturned towards the sun, is my lifestyle, by choice. It is said that I tend to have a bubbly, sunny disposition. In other words, being intentionally cheerful, optimistic, upbeat, cooperative, encouraging and motivated, with a ready smile on my face and a song in my heart, is my usual choice of mindset. That is correct. I said, it is my choice of mindset. Just like a remote control for the TV, I set my mind daily on all that is positive and productive. The same can be true for you if that is your decision. In this age where one's brand is one's life or business, did you ever think about what your brand is? Oh, you don't need to have a business to have a brand, for your brand is everything you are, everything you say, everything you do and everything you believe. It is what you show others day in and day out. As they say in Hollywood, "image is everything." What do people know about you? Are you upbeat and productive, or always finding fault with something or someone? Are you accepting of your responsibility for where you are in life, or are you blaming everyone else for your plight? As it is often said, "every tub has to stand on its own four feet," so let us choose to brand ourselves and our lives with the joie de vie, or joy of life, as well as the attitude of gratitude that we all were designed for.

Since our greatest power is to choose, we must set our minds daily, by expressing gratitude to God upon awakening as we count our blessings; by praying, listening to the wisdom He imparts; by reading a portion of scripture in order to properly guide our steps during the day; and by choosing to take one moment at a time, inspired to solve problems, rather than letting problems drown us in a multitude of "Oh poor me, woe is me, life is so bad and so sad" pity parties.

Having an attitude of gratitude is fundamental to the joy and good health that keeps a person buoyant.

True joy is not based on the circumstances of the day, for circumstances can be misleading. For example, I've seen people who appear, on the surface, to have the most enviable life: the best career, the best car, the most wonderful house, many expensive, material possessions and even fame, yet I have witnessed their expressed laments about the emptiness they found awaiting them at the zenith of their climb to the top. Conversely, joy is a direct result of living in God's presence. I know this because He is my Anchor. He keeps me afloat in the ocean of life. Yes, difficulties come and they go. When I stay in daily, active communication with the Lord, some problems resolve themselves and others I learn to deal with to get them resolved. Through it all, God is with me, assisting me with situations as I remain close to Him. He is my lifeline, my life jacket and as such, His joy is my strength, enabling me to have a sunny disposition. I often reflect on hymns and the following passages from the Bible, my GPS, which I reference often in my writing from either the King James Version or the New International Version, so those scriptures are usually noted as Book Name 3:17-19. For example, here are two of my favorite passages, the first noted in Habakkuk, chapter 3, verses 17-19, and the second is from Psalm 63:1-8. Both are certainly applicable to this discussion, as they express my purpose. May they also express yours.

"Though the fig tree does not bud and there are no grapes on the vines, though the olive crop fails and the fields produce no food, though there are no sheep in the pen and no cattle in the stalls, Yet I will rejoice in the Lord, I will be joyful in God my Savior. The Sovereign Lord is my strength; He makes my feet like the feet of a deer, He enables me to go on the heights." NIV

O God, Thou art my God; early will I seek Thee: my soul thirsteth for Thee, my flesh longeth for Thee in a dry and thirsty land, where no water is; To see Thy power and Thy glory, so as I have seen Thee in the sanctuary. Because Thy loving kindness is better than life, my lips shall praise Thee. Thus I will bless

Thee while I live: I will lift up my hands in Thy Name. My soul shall be satisfied as with marrow and fatness; and my mouth shall praise Thee with joyful lips: when I remember Thee upon my bed, and meditate on Thee in the night watches. Because Thou hast been my help, therefore in the shadow of Thy wings will I rejoice. My soul followeth hard after Thee: Thy right hand upholdeth me. – Psalm 63:1-8 KJV

No matter what curve balls life throws at me, I will rejoice in the Lord, for He is my Savior, my Deliverer, my Defense, my Refuge, my Help and my Advocate Who prays for me. This knowledge and reality is just as vital to me as having my GPS, also known as the Global Positioning System, when I am traveling, in order to take the best route to my destination, for this is a common practice. You see, our attitude totally determines our altitude, and impacts those who we encounter during the day. As we stay prayed up and praised up with the Lord, our attitude, our perspective and our performance rise higher. Sure, the tough times certainly come our way just as they do in everyone else's life. However, the difference is that our focus must be on God in order to make it through life's many trials. My focus is on the Lord because He saved me and gave me a great leg up on life. So with Him, every day can be the best day ever if I will continue to trust in Him, rely on Him and let my light shine for Him as I go about my day. Live Sunny Side Up with Christ. He can help you, improve your life and enable you to view life through the prism of hope.

Always Live Sunny Side Up!

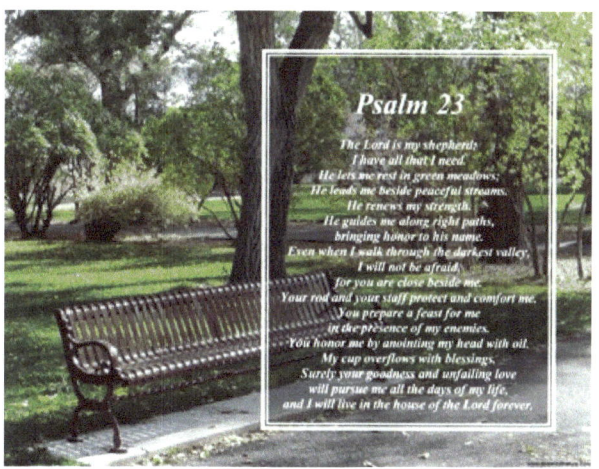

In Green Pastures, By Still Waters

The beloved twenty third psalm is one of the most popular scripture passages. For me, it is a love letter, full of promises that speak to, and comfort my heart, written by the psalmist David, by holy inspiration from The Lord. Above is one version of this popular passage in plain English. At the end of this chapter, you will find the traditional King James Version. However, allow me to share the Amplified Bible version, which clarifies or unpacks the basic understanding of this powerful, meaningful psalm which we shall discuss.

Psalm 23   Amplified Bible (AMP)

A Psalm of David.

[1] The Lord is my Shepherd [to feed, guide, and shield me], I shall not lack.

[2] He makes me lie down in [fresh, tender] green pastures; He leads me beside the still *and* restful waters.

³ He refreshes *and* restores my life (my self); He leads me in the paths of righteousness [uprightness and right standing with Him—not for my earning it, but] for His name's sake.

⁴ Yes, though I walk through the [deep, sunless] valley of the shadow of death, I will fear *or* dread no evil, for You are with me; Your rod [to protect] and Your staff [to guide], they comfort me.

⁵ You prepare a table before me in the presence of my enemies. You anoint my head with [a]oil; my [brimming] cup runs over.

⁶ Surely *or* only goodness, mercy, *and* unfailing love shall follow me all the days of my life, and through the length of my days the house of the Lord [and His presence] shall be my dwelling place.

One of my Favorite Psalms

Why is Psalm 23 one of my favorite psalms?

A. It speaks to my heart and answers my innermost questions by explaining how He meets all my spiritual needs, which in turn, also address my emotional, mental, physical and psychological needs.

B. It shows me how deeply The Lord loves and cares for me.

C. It teaches me how valuable having an intimate relationship with Him is and promises me that when I remain close to my Shepherd, He gives me His protection and comfort.

D. It is memorable, with only six verses that explain our direct relationship with our Heavenly Father, God, also called Abba.

E. It satisfies my deep love for literature, for this psalm tells a story and is complete with a plot, characterization, similes, metaphors and action. In fact, this psalm is a testimony that shares about God's deep personal love for us and His undying compassion.

F. It shows God's Holiness, Provision, Presence and Power.

Now let us look at and unpack the significance of the powerful words in this twenty-third psalm.

¹The Lord is my Shepherd [to feed, guide, and shield me], I shall not lack.

What does Lord mean, and what is meant if someone does not call Jesus Christ Lord?

In the New Testament of The Bible, the word, *Lord*, is the most frequently used title for Jesus Christ. Although people rarely use this term in their daily lives, we are all very familiar with another popularly used word, namely, boss. Basically, in plain language, that is what the word *Lord* means, for it refers to Jesus Christ Who has authority, power, and control in the Christ follower's life. The Bible, or The Word of God, also describes Jesus as the Head of the church, the Ruler over all creation, and the Lord of lords and King of kings (Col. 1:15–18; Rev. 3:14, 17:14). The full extent of Jesus Christ's reign covers everything in human life that happens in heaven and on the earth. No person, not even those who deny His existence, is free of His rule and no one is outside His sphere of authority. Although the enemy of Christ, Satan, daily tries to convince us that all liberty is found in doing whatever we want, when we want and how we want, actually, true freedom is only acquired through total submission to Christ's loving lordship.

Even death does not release us from the authority of God's only Son, for Jesus Christ is Lord of those who are living, as well as those who are dead. Everyone who ever lived, is alive now, or who will live in the future must decide to either lovingly accept and welcome Christ into their lives as Savior and Lord, or choose to rebel against our Savior, Who willingly gave His life then rose from the dead on our behalf so that we all may live forever. Each person has the opportunity to make this choice **only** while they are still living. After death, everyone will have to acknowledge Christ's lordship through accountability to Him for everything that was done during their life. If we have not chosen to bow the knee to Jesus in life, we will be forced to bend it in the Judgment.

Have you chosen to accept and submit to Christ's rule over your life? His authority often causes either fear or anger in people who have not yet chosen to yield to Him. However, those who have experienced His faithfulness, His help and deliverance, His loving kindness, trusted in His daily goodness, and surrendered to His authority take comfort in knowing Him as the Lord of their lives.

So, in the light of this foundation of understanding, let us examine the significance of the 23rd Psalm.

What is a shepherd?

A shepherd is one employed in tending, feeding and guarding the sheep. Jesus, the Good Shepherd, indicates the kind of shepherd He is. He, unlike some who would flee when facing danger, gave up His life for the sheep in His care. Second, His sheep know His voice, listen to Him and follow Him as the Book of John, chapter 10, verses 11 and 14 state.

Shepherd also means that Jesus Christ is personal, not some distant figure, and He has the priority and authority in the believer's life. To that, some people in this day and age would defiantly say, "You're not the boss of me," which is what rebels say to any authority figure when they tell them to do something. These days, there is a terrible defiance, total opposition and utter disregard for any authority figure. As an educator, this is particularly sad to observe for it is typified in the antisocial personality disorder, also known as APD, which is a diagnosis of those who routinely behave with little or no regard for authority, nor the feelings, rights and safety of others. It can surface in those who act as if they have no conscience, who act with predatory tendencies and have no concern about the consequences of their actions since they do not understand feelings of remorse and guilt, typically using deceit and manipulation in their interpersonal relationships.

However, Jesus takes care of and looks after His sheep who choose to follow Him. His sheep are the people of this world who have accepted Him and believe He will take of them. Sheep are completely reliant on the shepherd to take them to where there is food and protect them from wolves and other predators that would enjoy devouring a vulnerable sheep that was left unprotected. The sheep in Jesus' flock do need not fear anything for He has never lost a sheep that was placed in His care.

In the beloved twenty third psalm, God is using the analogy of sheep and their nature to describe each of us. What do you know about sheep? Well, I know that sheep have a natural tendency to wander off and get lost. As believers, we tend to do the same thing. It's as Isaiah 53:6 has said: "We all, like sheep, have gone astray, each of us has turned to his own way." Now when sheep go astray, they are in grave danger of getting lost, unable to find their way back safely, being attacked, or even killing themselves by drowning or falling off cliffs.

Likewise, within our own human nature, Romans 7:5 and Romans 8:8 explain that there is a strong tendency to go astray, either by pursuing the pride of life, noted by I John 2:16, or following the lusts of our flesh and eyes. "All we like sheep have gone astray" (Isaiah 53:6). "What man having a hundred sheep, if he lost one . . . will go after that which was lost" (Luke 15:4). Clearly, we are like sheep wandering away from Jesus Christ, the Shepherd through our own futile self-remedies and feeble attempts at self-righteousness. Hebrews 2:1 states that it is our nature to drift away, to reject God, and to break His commandments, such as in the previous paragraphs regarding APD. When we do this, we run the risk of getting lost, even forgetting the way back to God. Furthermore, when we turn away from the Lord, we soon find ourselves confronting many enemies who will attack us in devastating ways.

The bottom line is that we are described as sheep because we are basically helpless creatures who cannot survive long without a shepherd, upon whose care we are completely dependent. Therefore we are totally dependent upon the Lord to shepherd, protect, and care for us. Sheep are essentially dumb animals that do not learn well and are extremely difficult to train. They do not have good eyesight nor do they hear well. They are also known to be very slow animals who are totally unable to escape their predators since they have no camouflage and no weapons for defense such as claws, powerful jaw or sharp hooves.

In what other ways are we likened to sheep?

We satisfy self. Sheep will only eat what is in front of them.

We have no sense of danger. Sheep have no instinct to warn them of snakes, wolves, bears, parasites or any other predator.

We are defenseless. Sheep have no weapons to defend themselves, no claws, teeth, fangs, etc. "The wolf catcheth them" (John 10:12).

We are unaware. "As a sheep before a shearer is dumb" (Isa. 53:7).

We are the target of the enemy, Satan. "Grievous wolves shall enter, not sparing the flock." (Acts 20:29).

Why is the Lord likened to a shepherd?

a. He knows us. "I am the good Shepherd, and know My sheep, and am known of mine." (John 10:14).

b. He relates to us. "He calleth His own sheep by name and leadeth them out and when He putteth forth His own sheep, He goeth before them and the sheep follow Him, for they know His voice" (John 10:3,4).

c. He loves the sheep. "He (Jesus) was moved with compassion on them, because they were scattered abroad, as sheep having no shepherd" (Matt. 9:36).

d. He provides for the sheep. "I am come that they might have life, and have it more abundantly" (John 10:10).

e. He sacrifices for the sheep. "The good shepherd giveth his life for the sheep" (John 10:10). "I lay down my life for the sheep" (John 10:15).

f. He protects the sheep. "Thy servant (David) kept his father's sheep, and there came a lion, and a bear, and took a lamb out of the flock: and I went after him . . . and caught him by his beard, and smote him, and slew him" (I Sam. 17:34,35).

g. He feeds the sheep. "Thou preparest a table before me in the presence of mine enemies" (Ps. 23:5).

Summary: Therefore, your relationship with God is not a prize to be won, rather, it is a gift to be received.

C. I SHALL NOT WANT

1. What does the word "shall" mean to me?

a. Purpose of the will. I can make definite plans about the future. This is a word of intention.

b. Faith-desire. I expect the Lord to take care of me. "Whatsoever ye shall ask in prayer, believing, ye shall receive" (Matt 21:22).

c. Future state. I know the Lord will care for me. "Faithful is he that calleth you, who also will do it" (I Thess. 5:24).

C. I SHALL NOT WANT

2. What shall we "not want?"

a. What are the four greatest "wants" in life?

(1) Love me. "He gave His love to us" (Rom. 5:8).

(2) Accept me. "He that comes to me, I will not cast out" (John 6:37).

(3) Exalt me. "Whosoever therefore shall humble himself . . . the same is the greatest" (Matt. 18:4).

(4) Protect me. "My sheep . . . no one shall take them from Me" (John 10:27,28).

Jesus has declared that He is our Shepherd and demonstrated it by giving His life for us. Matthew 20:28 says, "The Son of Man did not come to be served, but to serve, and to give His life a ransom for many." Through His willing sacrifice, the Lord made salvation possible for all who come to Him in faith, according to John 3:16. In proclaiming that He is the good shepherd, Jesus speaks of "laying down" His life for His sheep in John 10:15,17-18.

Just like sheep, we need a shepherd because all mankind is spiritually blind and lost in their sin. This is why Jesus, in Luke 15:4-6, spoke of the parable of the lost sheep explaining that He is the Good Shepherd who laid down His life for each of us. He searches for us when we're lost, to save us and to show us the way to eternal life as clarified by Luke 19:10. Often we tend to be like sheep, so consumed with worry and fear, following blindly behind one another. John 10:27 says that by not following or listening to the Shepherd's voice, we can be led astray so easily by others to our own destruction. Jesus, the Good Shepherd, warns those who do not believe and listen to Him in John 10:25-28: "I did tell you, but you do not believe . . . you do not believe because you are not my sheep. My sheep listen to my voice; I know them, and they follow me. I give them eternal life, and they shall never perish; no one can ever snatch them out of My hand."

In the first three verses of Psalm 23 we learn that the Shepherd meets the sheep's every need: food, water, rest, safety, and direction. When we as believers follow our Shepherd, we know that we will have all we need. We know, according to personal experiences and The Holy Bible in Luke 12:22-30 that Jesus keeps His promises that we will not lack the necessities of life, for He knows exactly what we need.

² He makes me lie down in [fresh, tender] green pastures; He leads me beside the still   and restful waters.

Did you know that sheep will not lie down when they are hungry, nor drink from fast-flowing streams? Sometimes the shepherd will temporarily dam up a stream so the sheep can quench their thirst. Psalm 23:2 speaks of leading the sheep "beside the quiet [stilled] waters." The shepherd must lead his sheep because they cannot be driven. Instead, the sheep hear the voice of their shepherd and follow him, just as we listen to our Shepherd, Jesus Christ, in reading and studying His Word, The Bible, and following Him obediently by our choice of actions, according to John 10:3–5,16,27. And if a sheep does wander off, the shepherd will leave the flock in charge of his helpers and search for the lost animal (Matthew 9:36).

In Psalm 23:3, the Hebrew word translated "paths" means "well-worn paths or ruts." In other words, when sheep wander onto a new path, they start to explore it, which invariably leads them into trouble. This passage is closely akin to the warning in Hebrews 13:9: "Do not be carried away by all kinds of strange teachings," as stated by Apostle Paul in Ephesians 4:14.

Moreover, the shepherd cares for the sheep because he loves them and wants to maintain his own good reputation as a faithful shepherd. As we've seen in Psalm 23, the analogy of the Lord as the Good Shepherd was also applied by Jesus in John chapter 10. In declaring that He is the shepherd of the sheep, Jesus is confirming that He is God. The Eternal God is our Shepherd. We shall not want what the Shepherd gives because He takes care of everything we need, hence His Name, Jehovah Jireh, meaning "my provider." However, this does not mean that we can take our Lord Shepherd for granted, which applies to the following statements:

I want fun, since He gives satisfaction.
I want to fulfill my lust, since He cannot tempt us.
I want money, since He gives what money buys.
I want better circumstances, since He gives abundant life.
No, no, no, this is not how life should go in order for us to grow. Instead, let us remember the following verse which clarifies what our Shepherd does for us:

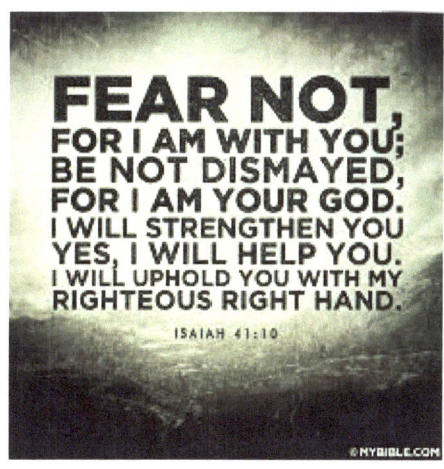

Therefore, let us pray the Twenty-Third Psalm:

> Precious Lord,
> Because You are my Shepherd,
> I commit all my needs to You. Please
> Provide green pasture for me to lie in, and
> Lead me beside still waters.
>
> Restore my soul when I am empty,
> Lead me in the right paths for Your Name's sake.
> Be with me in danger when I walk
> Through the valley of the shadow of death.
>
> Deliver me from evil
> And protect me with Your rod and staff.
>
> Prepare a table to feed me.
> So my enemies can see Your full provision.
> Anoint me with the oil of Your healing.
> Let me drink from the full cup of Your provision.
>
> Surely goodness and mercy will always follow me,
> And Lord, I want to live with You forever.

If you have never really accepted Jesus as your personal Savior, would you do it right now? Do not delay or put it off. If you would like to receive Christ by faith, pray this simple prayer in your heart:

Dear Lord, I acknowledge that I am a sinner. I believe Jesus died for my sins on the cross, and rose again the third day. I repent of my sins. By faith I receive the Lord Jesus as my Savior. You promised to save me, and I believe You, because You are God and You cannot lie. I believe right now that the Lord Jesus is my personal Savior, and that all my sins are forgiven through Your precious blood. I thank You, dear Lord, for saving me. In Jesus' name, Amen.

If you prayed that prayer, God heard you and saved you. I personally want to welcome you to the family of God. Please contact me at http://theauroralighthouse.com/ and tell me about your salvation experience so that I can rejoice with you.

Duh, I Don't Get It

OK, but what does all of this really mean? I still don't get it. Well, let me break it down further.

"The Lord is my Shepherd, I shall not want. He makes me lie down in green pastures, He leads me beside quiet waters, He restores my soul. He guides me in paths of righteousness for His Name's sake," as shared in the twenty-third Psalm, in the first two verses.

Now what do these words from David's beautiful pastoral song mean? In the twenty-third chapter of Psalms, the psalmist David describes the positive blessings belonging to all of God's people. The picture presented is one which is often witnessed in the shepherding valleys, where a flock of sheep, on a summer day or evening, are relaxing by the serene banks of a quiet stream. Along with their ever present Shepherd, these sheep also have in abundance all around them, the two main necessities or essentials of the gentle sheepfold, namely grass and water.

Did you know that the typical Eastern or Arabian shepherd is known to wander for many days, tirelessly seeking until he finds these requisite supplies for the docile sheep? Even the greenest grass would be insufficient without the stream, and even the purest water would be useless if it flowed through foul weeds, barren moorlands, or among dangerous rocks. In these two lovely, expressive emblems of this psalm, the Great Shepherd has made available the comforts and nourishment of His flock. In simpler terms, the ample supply of grace provided to the believer in the new covenant is designed to meet all of his or her spiritual needs. "He makes me to lie down in green pastures" means He makes me lie down in the pastures of tender grass. "He leads me beside the still waters" means He leads me beside the waters of quietness. Herein are clear thoughts for quiet reflection and meditation on the significance of this in our daily lives.

"He makes me to lie down in green pastures." The first idea suggested by this passage is rest, which also includes security. The words in the verse, "lie down," indicate a perfect relaxed repose in full security, without a single care. By nature, sheep are often extremely timid. In fact, to pass by them in a meadow is usually the signal for scattering the entire flock of sheep. However, any concern for fear or danger seems completely removed by the Presence of our Redeemer, Jesus Christ. Not a single bleat from the sheep is heard in all of the valley, for they are safely nestled, like little babies safe in their quiet cribs, as they are gathered around the feet of the True Shepherd.

Often, the human life is such an incessant striving after rest, wealth, success, possessions, health, security and satisfaction, with rest often being the primary pursuit. So many people are seeking these things in counterfeit pursuits, mere shadows of the real thing, aspiring for something tangible, noble and real. While chasing after shadows, there is the realization of a deep longing for what is really real. As Mick Jagger sang so popularly, "I can't get no satisfaction." This may well be the theme song for this incessant striving. The pleasure hunter seeks it in artificial, temporary excitements. The student seeks it in the loftier goals and achievements of his intellect. The thrifty pennypincher seeks it in the hoarding of his savings. The raving beauty seeks it in the endless acts to resurrect that which so often fades away as the years and countless operations enact their due justice. So many people seek it in so many different ways, yet true rest can only be found in Almighty God, our Heavenly Father. This is the real refreshment often symbolized by a rushing waterfall. This is the real repose, the sweet retreat, in which The Lord Almighty causes the weary to rest with satisfaction of refreshment. When the great I AM gives rest and quiet to His people, He gives His beloved the blessing of sleep, wherein they find rest and refreshment.

Only when we have secured the Divine Shepherd's love, pardon, favor and reconciliation through the atoning work of Jesus, our Redeemer, only then can we find rest in Him. Nothing else can satisfy this need, without Christ in our lives, for He is our Help, Peace and Eternal Rest.

The concept of green pastures also suggests that there is abundant provision in the Presence of The Lord. Notice that the verse does not specify only one piece of pasture, or meadow. Quite the contrary, for the plural form, "pastures" is used. This clearly shows that there is no shortage of what is needed. Rather, there is an amplitude, enough to meet the needs of every member of the flock. The sheep may roam from field to field, yet still there is more than enough and plenty to spare. Additionally, the provision of the pastures is the best of its kind, filled with young and tender grass, no charred nor bitter pieces anywhere in sight. It is as if an eternal spring or summer hovers over these meadows. What profound diversity and abundance there is in Father God's spiritual provision for His people!

There is even grace, sufficient for all times, every time. Each tender blade has its dewdrop full of comfort and every pool in the still waters shows its own reflection of God's amazing love. So many countless multitudes have been nourished by these pastures in every age and season of life, yet they are still green, in fact they are evergreen, or green forever. This is why the song of the flock still to this day is what it has been for three thousand years, "The Lord is my Shepherd, I shall not want (I long for nothing or I lack nothing.)"

This is also particularly true of the pastures of God's Holy Word! What variety we have here; comfort, inspiration, doctrine, precept, promise, poetic meditations, and everlasting consolation. At no time are these pastures greener to us than in seasons of sorrow, despair, and anguish. When the woes of the world attempt to consume us, it is then that it seems that those pastures that used to be carpeted with flowers and bathed in sunshine no longer offer us any refreshment or rest. Yet we must realize that although "the grass withers, and the flower fades, but the Word of our God shall stand forever." We can trust in that reality.

Now as we proceed to the second part of the verse, "He leads me beside the still waters." Still waters! These words appear to convey, under another figure and symbol, a description just of the same calm, holy, tranquil repose, secured to the believer, which the psalmist had in his mind in the preceding clause, the soul kept in perfect peace for it is stayed or focused on Almighty God. The wicked are compared to the "troubled sea" but this is an inland river with a quiet, gentle stream, protected from the boisterous winds which trouble the ocean to madness. Strange, indeed, often is the history of the soul before it attains that divine repose; fierce are its struggles before there ensues the calm of victory and rest. Like the patriarch at Jabbok before he secured the change of name and the divine blessing, it has often times been a long night of wrestling before the dawning of the day.

You may have witnessed such a peaceful meadow as that described by the psalmist of Israel, with its quiet, lake-like stream; so still, that not a ripple bedims its surface; every rock, and plant, and spear of grass, which fringe its banks, beautifully mirrored in the surface. Yet follow that same river up these mountain ravines, and you see it fretting and foaming over rugged rocks, hurrying impetuously down to where it now sleeps so calmly in the lower valley! That is a picture of the often long unrest of the soul before it has found the peace which passes understanding; its struggles with inward corruption and outward temptation; the fierce eddying currents and those impetuous cataracts of passion and sin, before it secure its glorious repose in God. Not until it reaches these quiet meadows, with their green pastures, which we have been now describing, can it say, "Return unto your rest, O my soul!"

Here, too, as in the former example, we have the abundance of God's mercies set forth; not only varied pastures but varied waters. The blessings of grace are not like the Nile, one solitary river which receives no tributary all the nine hundred miles it traverses. They are rather like the Jordan, fed by a hundred rills, as it hurries through its rocky gorges. Many streams only flow in winter or spring. When summer comes, the time they are most needed, their channels are dry. But these "still waters" are full even in drought, for they are fed from the everlasting hills. When the world's streams are emptiest, the streams of grace are deepest and most ample. "The Lord," says the prophet, "shall guide you continually, and satisfy your soul in drought, and make fat your bones; and you shall be like a watered garden, and like a spring of water whose waters fail not." We have streams of peace, of purity, of pardon, of righteousness, which are all exceedingly great and precious. Observe the splendor and exuberance of God's mercies in creation. Go to some peaceful garden of tangled loveliness, by a river, a brook, or waterfall, or a meadow. Study for an hour that one volume of nature, taking your microscope with you to help you see every glorious detail. How exquisite the hues and arrays of color! How perfectly symmetrical the forms of foliage and wildlife are! How lavish the architecture of the tiny insect worlds, all so very animated! It is a very minute type of the exceeding riches of His grace, all shown to us in His kindness extended through Jesus Christ. "Oh Lord, how great is Your goodness and blessings which You have laid up for those who fear You, which You have worked for those who trust in You!"

Some may incorrectly conclude from the reflection suggested by both phrases, that religion is happiness. The loveliest emblems in nature, "green pastures" and "still waters," are here combined to symbolize the experiences, and depict the reality, of the believer's life. The world has its pleasures too, and we do not affirm that they are devoid of attractiveness. Had this been the case, they would not be so fondly and eagerly held onto as they are. Still we can affirm, that while they are certain, sooner or later, to perish, they are fitful and capricious even while they last. They are built on sand, soon to washed away in the life oceans' tide, not built on the rock of faith which will stand no matter what life may toss its way. They are, at best, but the passing gleam of the meteor; not like the Christian's happiness, True Joy, founded in the enduring intimate Relationship with our Lord and Savior, Jesus Christ the Messiah. With Him, all of the exquisite joys of the true faithful believer far outlive all others, by the faithfulness, mercy, grace, provision, Presence, guidance and the unfailing, unsurpassed love in Jesus, our Divine Shepherd.

Come now, wandering one, enter within these all providing gates! Test for yourself the reality of the Divine Assurance: "The Name of the Lord is a strong tower; the righteous run into it and they are safe." Come now, wandering sheep! Prove the truthfulness as well as beauty of reclining on green pastures, and by still waters. Go and take your long awaited, long sought for, abiding rest and safety in those blissful, satisfying meadows of peace, kindness and sanctuary.

Note that this is rest in God and rest in the blessed assurance of His favor, yet it is not rest from the activities of a holy lifestyle. It is not rest or a vacation from a perpetual battle with sin. Thus, Christianity is not a condition of selfish nor passive inaction. The believer is a selfless steward, a servant with a heart for ministry, a diligent worker, a member of that royal priesthood who each respectfully has their own special ministry of responsibility and love in the work of the Kingdom. So, precious reader, allow this rest to be yours also, the purest rest which follows the purposeful consciousness born from The Lord of doing good, living justly, walking humbly with our God, loving mercy, demonstrating His unfailing love to all who seek the Divine Shepherd of our souls.

We value most the rest of the body when it is the recompense or compensation of hard work and longterm toil. He who has worked through the day the most bravely, sleeps most sweetly. Have you ever felt the sweetness of this rest? The pleasure experienced after some act of kindness, and compassion, and generous self-sacrifice, by which your fellows have been made the better and the happier, and in the doing of which you have been enabled, in some feeble degree, to imitate the example of Him whose life was a combination of duty and love? If these deeds are performed quietly and unostentatiously, so much more is it in accordance with the spirit of Christianity, and with the spirit of the emblem we have been now considering, the still waters, fringed with green, flowing gently, noiselessly, unobtrusively along, manifesting their presence only by the fertility they spread around them. Beautiful picture of the true Christian! The silent flow of life's everyday current, carrying blessings in its course, fertilizing as it flows the green border of faith and love, kindness, goodness, joy, patience, peace, meekness, charity and unselfishness.

Still waters also indicate depth. It is the shallow stream, much like the empty wagon, that makes the most hollow noise, gurgling and fretting along its pebbly channel. It is in God's grace as in nature, the gentle dew distills on the tender grass, the gentle rain feeds the mountain streams, and both of these imperceptibly feed the still waters in the lower meadows. Blessed resort, this sheltered valley of Christ's amazing love! Can't you hear Him calling you lovingly and patiently, as He gently beckons you, uttering the invitation, "Come unto me, and I will give you rest."

Once you have found the Shepherd of these green pastures and still waters, earnestly avoid everything that would lead you away from Him, and cause you to forfeit the possession of His favor and fond regard. It is the short but touching epitaph frequently seen in the catacombs at Rome, "In Christ, in peace." Therefore, realize the Holy Presence of The Divine Shepherd.

Be ever near these waters of quietness. Let the current of your daily walk and business run side by side with the heavenly stream. In this world you may be and must be. "In the world," says He, "you shall have tribulation (or trouble), but in Me you shall have peace." Moreover, when you come to the time to die, where others may speak of the worries of death, to you it will only be fulfillment under the guidance of our great Forerunner Jesus Christ, Who said, "When you pass through the waters, I will be with you." You will be in the arms of the Holy Shepherd, to rest forevermore in His celestial pastures, abiding blissfully with Him for all eternity. Hallelujah!

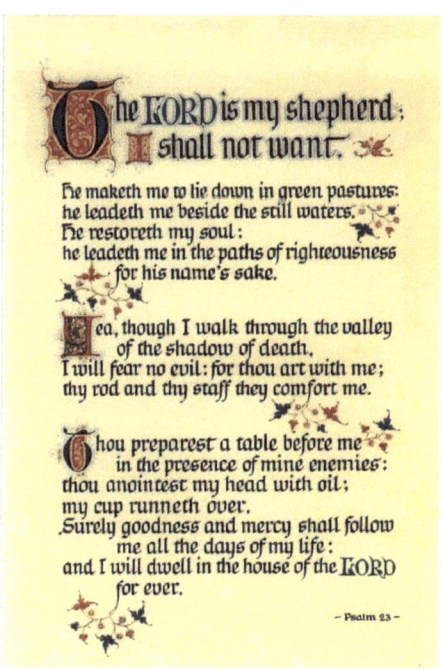

Finally, allow me to explain about the anointing the head with oil, as stated in verse 5 of this favorite passage. I realize that it may be difficult to understand for those living in a moderate climate where extreme heat seldom exists, yet in previous centuries, it was customary in severely hot climates to anoint the body with oil to protect it from excessive perspiration. When mixed with perfume, the oil imparted a delightfully refreshing and invigorating sensation. Athletes anointed their bodies as a matter of course before running a race. Even today, I notice that the fragrances I purchase that contain an oil base, have the most lasting fragrance which permeates my clothing and the area where I am working. This causes people to compliment me, particularly when there is a fan present, as the pleasant, light aroma wafts throughout the area. Therefore, just as the body that was anointed with oil was refreshed, energized, enabled, invigorated, and better fitted for action, so The Lord anoints His "sheep" with the Holy Spirit, Whom oil symbolizes, to enable them to engage more freely in His service and run in the way He directs, in heavenly fellowship with Him, in strengthening of His kingdom, and to the benefit of the communities in which the sheep serve. May we each be a pleasant fragrance to Him as we bloom where we are planted.

In His Holy Presence

Realize that Father God is nearer than you think, for He is richly present in all of our earthly moments, if we would just open our eyes. He is there in the sweet song of the diverse variety of morning birds, chirping in celebration of the new day and all that is provided for them. Just like He watches over them, He watches over you and me. We are connected to The Lord in bonds of love that are unsevered no matter what happens. Yet there are times when we feel alone as we go through life's temporary travails, since because of our human limitations, we cannot physically see our union with The Lord Who loves us more than life itself. Just ask Him to open your eyes so that you can find Him all the time, everywhere. As we grow in our awareness of His Holy Presence, we also grow in our feeling secure, safe and protected. There are those who will say that they do not need a "crutch" to lean on because of their great intellect. However, this is NOT an intellectual escape or any other sort of escape from reality. No, my dear reader, this is about learning to tune in to the true, ultimate reality, for Father God is more Real and Dear that anything we ca hear, see, fathom or touch in this earthly world. He is eternal and those who worship Him in Spirit and Truth will live with Him eternally. This is the reward of living by faith in Him, for faith is the confirmation of things we do not see. It is the conviction of their actual reality, for in faith, we perceive as real fact what is not revealed to our earthbound senses. Note the following scripture verses that confirm this.

Now faith is the assurance (the confirmation, the title deed) of the things [we] hope for, being the proof of things [we] do not see and the conviction of their reality [faith perceiving as real fact what is not revealed to the senses]. Hebrews 11:1 Amplified Bible

"God did this so that men would seek Him and perhaps reach out for Him and find Him, though He is not far from each one of us. 'For in Him we live and move an have our being.' As some of your own poets have said, 'We are His offspring." Acts 17:27-28

Practice His Presence

The Lord replied, "My Presence will go with you, and I will give you rest."   Exodus 33:14

Lord, You have taught me that in Your love, I have nothing to fear or be worried about. Today I rejoice that You are never changing, always the same yesterday, today and forever. I realize more each day just how much You really love me, as I reflect on Your complete commitment to totally investing Your life before, during, and after the cross on my behalf. That floors me. There are no words for the depths of love You daily demonstrate for me: watching over me while I sleep; providing sweet rest for my weary mind and body; awakening me to see a brand new day; giving me the activity of a right mind; granting me health, strength and mobility; enabling me to make sound, wise decisions; communicating with me and teaching me to honor You in all I do. All this and more that You do seamlessly, daily, just leaves me speechless. Such love is astounding!

One of the biggest things today that penetrates my understanding is my choice of what to focus on and the impact that choice has on each day's activities. For some reason, my mind tends to gravitate towards worrying instead of praying when I'm not concentrating on You and Your Word. When I focus on the problems, pressures and circumstances around me, I start to feel worried, alone and baffled. I become so caught up in the vortex of either worry or negativity that I stop praising You, stop praying and start worrying even more. However, when I choose to focus on You, fixing my eyes on Your unfathomable faithfulness, on how blessed I am because of You, on how You have already conquered the world on my behalf, and how deeply You surround me with Your Holy Presence, then that is when I come alive! I am amped up, readied by Your Strength, Your Power, Your Presence, Your Grace, Your Mercy, Your Joy. It is then that I realize that there is absolutely nothing impossible with my Savior, Master and Lord, my precious Redeemer, Jesus Christ.

Lord, I hear You within me, speaking to me as I sit at Your feet, "You are mine for all time, baby girl. Know that nothing can separate you from My Love. Since I invested My Life in you, you can be very well assured that I Will also take excellent care of you. So, whenever your mind goes into neutral or auto pilot, and your thoughts start to flow freely, that is when you tend to feel anxious and alone. You begin to act like the weight of the whole world is on your tiny shoulders. Your only focus becomes problem solving and you forget that you don't know everything. I do. Just relax in My Presence, baby girl. Let it go, let it all go and let Me handle all of it. Remember, I got this. Now, to get your mind back into the proper gear, just look to Me. Lay yourself down and lay all your problems down at My Feet. I got this. Many problems vanish instantly in the Light of My Love, because you finally realize that you are never, ever alone. Other problems may remain, but they all become secondary to knowing Me and rejoicing in the relationship I so freely offer you. In every moment of life, you can choose either to practice My Presence or you can choose to practice the presence of problems, which are only temporary.

That said, I choose in life to practice being still and focused on You in Your Presence, Lord, rather than to continue to practice being focused on the problems that everyday life generates. Greater is He Who is in me than he who is in the world. Problems do not govern my life, I govern my life by the thoughts and choices I make. Each moment I can either move forward in the progression of greatness the Lord has planned for me, or I can move backwards by wallowing in all of life's draining negativities of unproductive focus. I choose You, Most Heavenly Father God, You. You are my Oasis of rest and the fulfillment of every spiritual fruit that You are manifesting in me.

The Lord replied, *"My Presence will go with you, and I will give you rest."* Exodus 33:14

For I am convinced that neither death nor life, neither angels nor demons, neither the present nor the future, nor any powers, neither height nor depth, nor anything else in all creation, will be able to separate us from the love of God that is in Christ Jesus our Lord. Romans 8:38–39

Forgive Yourself

Don't be so hard on yourself when your mind wanders while you are praying, and do not get upset with yourself or be surprised about it. Know that it is all right to be human. Your weakness and brokenness are the windows that permit His Strength to permeate you as the Light and Knowledge of His Holy Glory shine in your life. Remember, His strength and power are more evident in your weakness. Just take a breath and turn your attention back to The Lord, just as you would turn your attention back to your best friend during a conversation after being temporarily distracted. You can rejoice in the love Father God has for you, for it is limitless and unconditional. Because of this, you can smile, basking in His loving warmth and understanding, for He is the Greatest Love of All. Whisper or speak His name reverently with loving contentment, with every assurance that He will never, ever leave or reject you. Take the time, make it a priority to think about Him throughout your day, realizing how awesome, excellent, marvelous, wonderful and amazing He and His Love are. As you do this, you are not only practicing His Presence, but you will be graced with a gentle, quiet spirit. This pleases Father God. Living in the Light of His glorious Presence comes from daily communion, or close communication, with The Lord. This filters through you and blesses others.

For God, Who said, "Let light shine out of darkness," made His light shine in our hearts to give us the light of the knowledge of the glory of God in the face of Christ. But we have this treasure in jars of clay to show that this all-surpassing power is from God and not from us.
2 Corinthians 4:6-7

Instead, it should be that of your inner self, the unfading beauty of a gentle and quiet spirit, which is of great worth in God's sight. 1 Peter 3:4

> [The Lord] said to me, My grace (My favor and lovingkindness and mercy) is enough for you [sufficient against any danger and enables you to bear the trouble manfully]; for My strength and power are made perfect (fulfilled and completed) and show themselves most effective in [your] weakness. Therefore, I will all the more gladly glory in my weaknesses and infirmities, that the strength and power of Christ (the Messiah) may rest (yes, may pitch a tent over and dwell) upon me! —2 Corinthians 12:9 AMP
>
> To him who is able to keep you from falling

Grieve and Rejoice

Recently my dear Christian friend passed away very suddenly. Even though I realized that she had gone home to heaven, the news hit me like a speeding Mac truck. I was so devastated that I closed the bedroom door and sobbed. Over the next weeks it is, was and always has been the Grace, Presence and Strength of The Almighty Lord that carries me through each day. Moment by moment, I trust and talk with Him. He is, was and always has been with me, never leaving me alone to deal with this new level of difficulty. Although I tried to stay focused by prayerful meditation and stay busy by working, at times an ocean of tears would rapidly come gushing out at the most inopportune moments. Yet along with the kindness of so many caring, wonderful people, I craved most of all some alone time, for it was in my times alone that I was able to draw so much strength and help from The Bible, God's Holy Word, as well as songs that lifted my weary spirit.

In the presence of others, my now limited energy was deeply drained and there just wasn't my usual joyful abundance to handle talking and being with others while I grieved, and even afterwards when I thought I should be able to move on with life. I found that when I'm working for short bursts of time, I'm better able to function. Also, the company and communication of those dear to my heart provided more wind beneath my wings. Yet even the slightest things like a fragrance, sight, word or song, brings up a waterfall of memories and joyful mourning.

As a Christian, I know how to live sunny side up. This intense, unprecedented, painful experience is a new chapter in my life, a time of very insightful, constructive development.

Today's Scripture

"The simple believe anything, but the prudent give thought to their steps."
Proverbs 14:15, NIV

Christians need a good theology of Christian death because it is critically important. Should we rejoice or weep when a brother or sister in Christ dies? Is a Christian funeral service a celebration or a time for mourning? One needs the right understanding of how to consider a Christian's death in order not to confuse these two extremes of merely rejoicing or merely grieving.

How routine it is to hear the heartfelt sentiment of a dear dying Christian say, "Don't weep when I die. Rejoice, for I shall be with Christ." With the same affection, it is normal to hear family members or friends of a deceased Christian say, "He/She didn't want us to grieve. We want to joyfully remember the life he had and remind ourselves that he is truly in a better place." Although these are endearing, well meant statements, I certainly don't want to disparage the affection that moved these sentiments. However, these responses are insufficient. We should not just rejoice when a Christian dies. Here are the reasons why.

As Romans 6:23 tells us, "The wages of sin is death." It is not a good thing that our Christian friend or family member has passed away. No matter the benefits after death, death *itself* is an abomination. Death is an unwelcomed guest. It had no place in creation. Rather, it stormed onto the scene as the thief of life upon the entrance of sin into this world. Therefore, death *itself* is not to be celebrated. We cannot just rejoice when a Christian dies, somehow forgetting that death is an enemy.

God formed man from the dust of the earth. Creation is turned on its head as man is returned to the dust in his death. There has been loss and that was not meant to be in this world. There has been death, which had no place in God's creation. In death, man is torn asunder, ripped in two. His body and soul, created as one person, are now separated. At that very moment when a Christian dies, the a Bible says that their soul immediately passes into the Presence of Christ, according to Philippians 1:23 and Luke 23:43, but their body is left to decay. While their soul is naked before the Lord, their body lies lifeless and devoid of the soul until the final resurrection. Therefore, there is a sense in which we could say that our naked souls are longing for the day of resurrection. For on that day, the souls will be reunited to their bodies, never to experience that horrible separation again. We will forever live as we were created to be.

You may remember some scriptures about Mary and Martha. Mary, Martha and their friends had good reason to weep at the loss of their brother Lazarus in John 11:33. Nowhere in The Holy Bible are Christians ever asked to deny their feeling of grief, for grief is a right and holy sadness. Also, we should never ask our loved ones to deny that emotion either. After all, according to John 11:32-35, when Jesus learned of Lazarus' death, He wept. Therefore, grief is a valid emotion that is supported by the teaching of the Bible.

However, we should not merely grieve. When a Christian dies we should also be filled with rejoicing. Truly, according to Philippians 1:21, for the Christian, "to live is Christ, and to die is gain." Moreover, in the 23rd verse, Philippians 1 explains that a believer in Christ who departs from this life is immediately in a far better place, for they are with Christ! They have finished the race and kept the faith (2 Timothy 4:7); and according to 2 Corinthians 5:7, that faith has become sight, for they no longer see in a mirror dimly, but see Christ face to face as stated by 1 Corinthians 13:12. Finally, Jesus Christ, the Object of their love, affection, joy and utmost adoration is now standing before them and is with them forevermore.

Wow! So many amazing glories await the Christian at death. In one moment, a feeble sinner saved by God's grace experiences the miseries of this life. In the next moment, that same person is adorned with the crown of righteousness, as 2 Timothy 4:8 shares, and standing in the Holy Presence of the King of Glory, Jesus Christ.

There the Christian shall be totally surrounded by His Awesome Glory, a Glory which banishes all of our enemies. In that place there will no longer be any experience of pain, loss, grief, discomfort nor regret. Instead, the saint shall live in sheer joy and bliss as they revel in the beauty and glory of their precious Savior and God forever. Therefore, let us rejoice at the death of a Christian, for as the Apostle Paul says in Philippians 1:23, they are "in a far better place." There may be no greater understatement ever written about all the marvelous glories that await us the followers of Jesus Christ!

Therefore, when a brother or sister in the Lord passes away, there should be grief and rejoicing. They both have their rightful place. We grieve for what is lost and we rejoice at what is gained. This then explains the proper responses to a Christian's death.

Sometimes people are so caught up in living that they fail to prepare for dying. Earlier, I focused on the scripture from Proverbs 14:15, that shares "the prudent give thought to their steps." One of the traits of a prudent person is that he or she gives serious thought to how they think, act and feel. Far too many people these days just let their emotions control everything they do. They let the media, their peers and the world around them dictate how they think, feel, dress and act. They believe everything they see and hear in the news, not realizing that much of it needs to be taken with a grain of salt to filter what's really true and relevant. If the news is bad, then they have a bad day. If the economy is down, they're down and when the economy is up, they're having a great day.

Please don't allow your life to be shaped in those ways. Make it a top priority in your life to give serious thought to your ways. Ask the Lord in prayer to guide your thoughts and decisions. Talk to Him about what's on your mind and whatever's troubling your heart. Don't believe everything you hear. Submit your life and concerns to Him. Ask Him to guide you. Proverbs says that when you submit your plans to The Lord, your ways will be established, He'll direct your steps, give you a phenomenal, supernatural peace and He'll bless you all the days of your life. He is faithful and good to those who seek Him and follow His direction. He's the best GPS you can ever have. Give thought to your life and seek the Lord!

A Prayer for Today

"Heavenly Father, thank You for Your faithfulness to me. Thank You for guiding and directing my steps. Help me to give thought to my ways every day and follow the good plan You have for me in Jesus' name. Amen."

The Audacity to Live

The following scripture speaks about your worth and mine. Listen to the personal guarantees:

The Lord your God is with you. He is mighty to save. He will take great delight in you. He will quiet you with His love. He will rejoice over you with singing. Zephaniah 3:17

What is your worth? What is the meaning of your life? You are worthy because you are loved.

The Lord is my haven of rest, my inspiration and my reason for living. I adore Him deeply and passionately, as I pray to know Him more intimately day by day, moment by moment as I grow in this life journey. May I resemble the One Who loves me so much that He gave Himself for me so that I could have a Bright Future, full of Hope, Help and Favor according to Jeremiah 29:11. Lord, help me to just be so real, so authentic, that others will see, feel and hear You in me. This is my prayer. Therefore, I chose the above scripture because it speaks to who and why we are. Word for word, here is what this verse means personally.

<u>The Lord Your God</u>: The Lord is **my** God, **my** Lord. I am His. He is mine. I ascribe or give to Him all the glory, all the majesty and all the praise that is due to Him. He is sovereign, omnipotent, all powerful and in full control of everything and everyone, including me and my life. After all, He paid the ultimate price for me…**His Life in my place**, and He rose from the dead to guarantee me eternal life with Him.

The Lord your God <u>is with you</u>: This means that God is right here with Me, little old me! Every single day, He holds my little hand, guiding me every little step of my life. He carries me when I am unable to walk on my own. He lives within me, speaking to me through various ways to inspire and help me stand strong. Whenever He seems silent, I know indubitably that He is always there because He promised me in His Word that He will never leave me, never forsake me and that His love is infinite. Therefore, there is nothing and no one that can separate me from His love, according to Romans 8.

<u>He is mighty.</u> The Almighty God is omnipotent, or all powerful, so much so that He is totally capable of anything that He wills or desires to do. He has promised to do good to those who love Him and who are called to fulfill His purpose in life according to Romans 8:38.

<u>He is mighty to save.</u> This means that He is the God who rescues and delivers me. He is my Hero, my Victor, my Champion Who saves me from my inevitable sin, from myself, from my overly self critical ways, ever from my mistakes. The Lord is a faithful warrior

And He has sanctified me, that is, He has set me apart just for His glory. I am designed by Him to fulfill His purposes on this earth wherever and however He has planted me among the lives of those He sent me here to be a blessing to. This is why I often say that I am blessed to be a blessing. My precious Lord redeems me and set me free to live, really live, without fear and condemnation. He even redeems me from my many mistakes, struggles, wonderings, wanderings, missteps and hardships, all of which He turns for good, using me to help others along the way. He tells me in His Word that I am so special (and you are too) that He has engraved us on the palms of His hands! This is how magnificent and endearing His love is for us.

<u>He will take great delight:</u> In other words, The Lord takes great pleasure and joy in……<u>In you:</u> in me and you!!! Wow, this means that no matter how many faults I have, He still loves me, and looks way beyond all of my faults to love me and meet my needs! In fact, I am the apple of His eye, as He expresses. Oh, how He loves you and me!

<u>He will quiet you</u>: means that He will give me rest, peace and calm my anxious thoughts.

<u>With His love</u>: Just knowing that He loves me infinitely and cares for me daily melts my heart and lifts my spirits. I am deeply reassured and encouraged that I am special to Him.

<u>He will rejoice</u>: The Lord will be ecstatic, overjoyed, and thrilled in full celebration. Why?

<u>Over you</u>: Because He loves you and me so much! He deems us as precious to Him.

<u>With singing</u>: My precious Lord sings for me and about me…amazing!!! He rejoices over me with love songs, just as a bridegroom rejoices about his bride. My Lord sings a pure, sweet song to cherish me, and the immensity of His love can only be measured by heaven's highest standards. Oh, how amazing is the depth of His love beyond man's understanding!!! What a cherished gift His love is, enabling us to live for He came to give us abundant life, according to John 10:10!

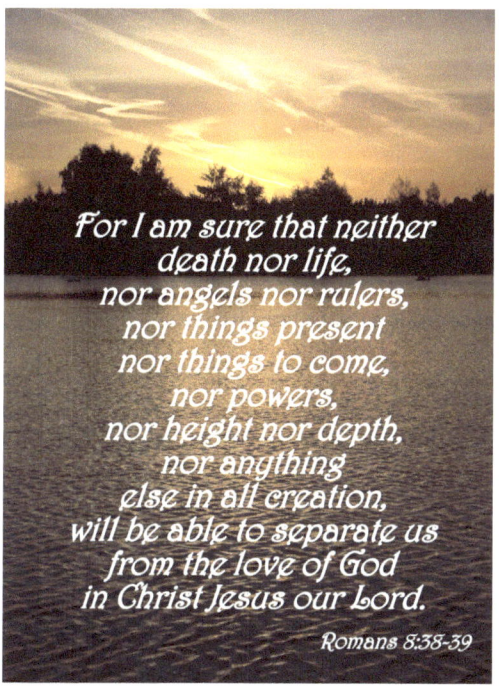

Transitions

There are times in life, no matter who you are, when it feels like you've leaped from the sizzling hot frying pan into the scorching, raging fire. Suffering, that is, being crushed and going through the squeeze as life's trials grind you through the pressure process, is a necessary part of life. Jesus Christ said, "In this world, you will have trials but be if good courage, I (Jesus Christ) have overcome the world. So when you are going through the Holy Refiner's Fire, which sharpens and strengthens you to become more like The Messiah, rejoice or as James 1 says, "count it all joy...so that patience (endurance) will have its perfect work (be completed in you).

While you are going through the fire, be confident that God is with you, like the three Hebrew boys in the Old Testament who were thrown into the fire for refusing to worship (bow down) before the king and his idol. They told him, in my own paraphrase here, that they serve The One True God and He is the only One they will worship, so do whatever you feel you have to do, for we know that God is with us. Now after a time, when the king and his guards were looking at the three teenage Hebrew boys, Shadrach, Meshach and Abednego (who I've often heard referred to as A Bad Negro to characterize the believer's toughness and resilience as they're going through their trials), the king and his men were shocked. They said that it looks like a Four men are in the fiery furnace and One looks like The Son of God. Hallelujah! So remember when you are going through, stay close to The Lord in prayer, praise and meditation on The Word of God so you can perceive the Presence of God:

For in sickness, God's healing shows up.

In pain and sorrow, God's comfort and mercy show up.

In persecution, God's help shows up.

In bondage to the past or anything else, God's deliverance shows up.

In the new level of promotion, where new devils try to slaughter your spirit, God's strength shows up.

Wherever God is, the Great I AM is there, making lemonade out of lemons, limeade out of limes, sweetness out of sour bitterness, beauty out of our ashes and sorrow, hope out of hopelessness, help in the helpless times, a brighter tomorrow out of a tough today and a better you through all the slaying and praying that you're going through.

Hang in there, God is not finished with you yet. Remember, everything that He taught you before that test or trial began, He is expecting to show up in you as the pressures of life squeeze it out of you.

So, don't think you're crazy as everything starts blowing up in your life and you start asking the Lord, with all kinds of doubts in your mind, "Did you really tell me to do this thing, listen to this person, move to this place, meet this person who just died suddenly, marry that person, start this new job, start this business, go on this faith journey? As the tears fall down your cheeks, the wind seems to go out of your sails and the unending questions roll through your mind to your lips, asking "Why?"...Do Not Despair. Instead, ask The

Lord, Our Potter Who repairs each of us cracked pots and chooses to use us for His Glory, "Why not me?"

Isaiah 41:10 New Living Translation (NLT)

ⁱ⁰ Don't be afraid, for I am with you.
Don't be discouraged, for I am your God.
I will strengthen you and help you.
I will hold you up with my victorious right hand.

Encourage yourself in The Word, speak over yourself the blessings and promises that The Lord has promised to His followers. Gird up your loins, straighten up your back, be determined and courageous, fellow warrior of faith. For God is with you, He promised in His Word never to leave you nor forsake you. He told us that Christians indeed will experience trials and suffering, but do not worry. He has already overcome on our behalf, for He's got your back and mine. He will bring you out of this whole, set free, better than ever, without the faintest hint of smoke from that raging fire you're dealing with.

Trust Him, just trust in The Lord. No, you are not alone as you go through what seems like hell on earth. Like me and anyone else, you are just going through the olive press. Just remember as you go through times of testing that God's perfect timing for breakthrough is coming in His own perfect time.

You see, you need to remember how the most precious thing in the world, olive oil, is made. Everyone in the cooking and health worlds often laud the benefits of extra virgin olive oil, but have you ever thought about how this most wonderful oil is made?

Three Essentials of Life

The Bible mentions three things in many scriptures: the grain, the wine and the oil. I wondered why the Lord always mentions these three items together. In studying His Word, the following became clear.

Through the grain, the wine and the oil, we can receive by grace alone, all the benefits of Jesus. These benefits cannot be obtained by any means of accomplishing or striving on our own, for in and of ourselves, we are insufficient. This is why we need Jesus Christ, our true Messiah. Man ate his way into trouble in the Garden of Eden. However, we can eat our way back into God's blessings by seeing our blessed Savior in The Grain, The Wine and The Oil. Allow me to explain.

The grain and the wine represent the Holy Communion, which speaks of the broken body of Jesus Christ and the blood that He shed to save you and me. In order to make bread, you take the wheat or the grain, then you must crush it and beat it in order to make dough. Next, to shape it, you must punch the dough, then put it into the fiery heat for an extended period of time in order for it to become bread. That is what happened to our Lord Jesus Christ on the cross. He was beaten severely, suffered greatly, bled profusely, endured fiery trials, died and rose again, on our behalf, in order to become our Bread of Life.

The Garden of Gethsemane

According to Matthew 26:36, the scriptures share: Then Jesus went with his disciples to a place called Gethsemane, and he said to them, "Sit here while I go over there and pray." Now, before our Lord's betrayal and arrest, he went to Gethsemane to pray. He took His disciples with Him, keeping some distance between them. Afterwards, Jesus Christ was betrayed by Judas Iscariot, was arrested in the garden, then taken away for trial and execution. I share this to explain that the word "Gethsemane" means "the oil press place." Gethsemane was an olive grove located on the Mount of Olives. In fact, its name suggests a place where the olives are processed into oil. Did you know that oil is a symbol of both the spirit and of understanding? In order to draw the oil from the olive, an oil press is used to cause great pressure on it. Jesus is the Olive Root, according to Romans 11:16, for He supports every olive branch and therefore every olive in the tree. He experienced enormous pressure in that place, so much so that the tremendous pressure that was upon Him can be seen to draw out liquid in Luke 22, fulfilling the meaning of the name, Gethsemane:

And being in anguish, He prayed more earnestly, and His sweat was like drops of blood falling to the ground.

The oil that is drawn or that exudes from our lives makes us useful to Almighty God. One of the purest forms of oil is extra virgin olive oil, which is transformed from freshly plucked olives.

Now, in order to make wine, the grapes not only have to be plucked from the vine, they also need to be crushed and stepped on. In the

Bible days, they said trodden upon. In the same manner, our blessed Savior Jesus Christ was trodden upon by the judgment of God for the sin of all mankind. Jesus chose to go through all that suffering for us to become the new wine of covenant, life and hope for all of us. Truly, Jesus saves. So do not worry, for now we see how the "press" that God has us in right now is truly designed to generate the purest of oil from our lives.

By the same token, olive oil, a necessity of life, is made from the olive fruit. When you press the fruit real hard, you will only find a white sap in stead of oil. Also, the fruit tastes very bitter. In order to get the precious olive oil, the fruit and its seed must be crushed by an immense weight in an olive press. The crushing also removes the bitterness. In the same manner, our blessed Jesus was crushed under the burden and weight of all of our sins, and also under the judgment of our Holy Father God. Christ was crushed to become the Anointing Oil that heals us. Let's take the time to understand more about the olive press process.

Our Heavenly Father God personally chose every single one of us long before He created the world. He knew what His purpose for each of our lives was before we were even conceived, in fact, each of our births was by His Holy Design, according to Jeremiah 1:5 NLT which states, *"I knew you before I formed you in your mother's womb. Before you were born, I set you apart…"*

This proves that each of us was handpicked by Father God to fulfill His purpose or mission in the world. How exciting and uplifting this is to know! Yet this is not all there is to the process of making oil from olives.

Next, the handpicked olives travel by conveyor belt to be washed, for without thorough cleaning, they are unfit to be used to make the purest oil. In correlation to our own lives, the redeeming blood of Jesus Christ cleanses us from all sin's impurities, as noted by I John 1:7 NIV, *"Bit if we walk in the light, as He is in the light, we have fellowship with one another, and the blood of Jesus, His Son, purifies us from all sin."*

Still, there is more to be done to make this pure olive oil. The olives and their pits are crushed into a paste. Do you understand that? Our pit is our core, the very essence of our being from which the issues of life flow, that is, the pit is our heart.

Proverbs 4:23 Amplified Bible (AMP)

²³ Keep and guard your heart with all vigilance and above all that you guard, for out of it flow the springs of life.

Once we, like olives, have been washed, we are ready to be crushed! It is during this phase of oil development that many lose sight of the ultimate goal and want to give up. **Do you feel like your heart has been crushed?** Does it seem like everything around you is falling down and crumbling right on top of you? **Well, give all praise to God for you are in the Olive Press and He is producing a profound anointing from your life that will bless others as well as you!** Trust me, I know firsthand, from experiencing three deaths of dearly loved ones within three months, that this process hurts, but hear me, this is NOT the time to jump out of the olive press! Hold on! Watch Father God reveal His glory.

Being Crushed in the Olive Press of Life

Much like the preparation of the grain, the wine and the oil, there are many situations in life that beat or crush us in the Olive Press, or the life pressures that we experience. However, we must remember to be joyful to be counted worthy of this process. As we endure, we know that God has promised us in Jeremiah 29:11, that He has plans to help us, not to harm us, plans to give us hope and a good future. So we can trust that, no matter what is going on, God is working in it and through it to bring good not only for our benefit, but also to help others. You see, when you come out of that trying experience whole and improved, you will be able to tell somebody else that they can make it through too. In other words, each one can reach one. So be encouraged: something better IS on the other side of that difficulty. Consider this verse from James 1:2.

Consider it all joy, my brethren, when you encounter various trials, knowing that the testing of your faith produces endurance...

This often quoted verse of scripture shares that we are to rejoice as we experience life's many trials, realizing that in the testing, or in the process of pressing, that our faith, when tested, will result in endurance, and he who perseveres will receive the crown of life promised by The Lord to all who love Him, as shared by James 1:12. Hang in there, for the best that The Lord has in store for you, is yet to come. *Precious Father God, Thank You for choosing me to fulfill Your purpose and deciding that I was worthy enough to go through some tough trials so that Your kingdom may be edified. I rejoice to be counted worthy to suffer for Your Holy Name. I ask that You fully equip me for my Olive Press Periods. Help me to deal with the pains and discomforts of those times. Lord, please give me the strength to stand firm throughout the process. May Your glory be revealed in and through me. In Jesus' matchless Name, Amen.*

Deep Waters
Vicki Evans/Aurora A. Ambrose

When I walk through deep waters
I know that You will be with me
When I'm standing in the fire
I will not be overcome
Through the valley of the shadow
I will not fear

I am never alone
No, I am never alone
You always go before me
You said You will never leave me

In the midst of my deep sorrow
I see Your light is breaking through
All the darkness of night won't overtake me
I am pressing and holding onto You
Lord, You fight my every battle
And I will not, shall not fear

I am never alone
No, I am never alone
You always go before me
You said You will never leave me

Lord, You amaze me
You Love and Redeem me
You even call me as Your own

Lord, You're my Strength
You're my Defender
You're my Refuge in this storm
Through all of these trials
You've always been faithful
You bring healing to my soul

I am never alone
No, I am never alone

You always go before me
You said You will never leave me
Selah. Think on this
Each time I do
It brings me bliss!
Vicki Evans/Aurora A. Ambrose

"You are the Song I'm Singing"
Colton Dixon

When I can't find the words to say how much it hurts
You are the healing in my heart
When all that I can see are broken memories
You are the light that's in the dark

You are the song
You are the song I'm singing
You are the air
You are the air I'm breathing
You are the hope
You are the hope I needed
Oh oh
You are

And when my circumstance leaves me with empty hands
You are the provider of my needs
When all my dirtiness has left me helpless
You are the rain that washes me

You are the song
You are the song I'm singing
You are the air
You are the air I'm breathing
You are the hope
You are the hope I needed
Oh oh
You are

It's Only Temporary

"For our light and momentary troubles are achieving for us an eternal glory that far outweighs them all." 2 Corinthians 4:17, NIV

Never, ever be surprised by all of the various fiery attacks on your mind, body, rest, peace and strength. While you are struggling to find help from Jesus, our Redeemer, and to live in His Abiding Peace, do not let discouragement set in.

Do you realize that you are often engaged in massive spiritual warfare? Well, if you are a follower of Jesus Christ, you are like the bulls' eye on a target. The evil one detests your total dependence on The Lord and your intimate closeness with Him, so he and his demonic underlings are ever determined to destroy that holy intimacy, which is the root of your joy. "The joy of the Lord is your strength."

Whenever you find yourself in the thick of battle, call upon His Holy Name: "Jesus, help me!" At that very instant, the battle belongs to The Lord. Now, your role is simply to trust Him as He fights for you. Your troubles and trials in this life are only temporary. In fact, these verses tell us they are momentary. Compared with eternity, our troubles do not last long at all. As you stand strong in faith during times of adversity, Scripture says that you are achieving eternal glory. When you confess your trust and reliance on God, you are passing the test!

Finally, realize that the Name of Jesus, properly, reverently and respectfully used, has unlimited Power to bless, heal, anoint and protect. At the end of time, *every knee will bow in heaven, on earth, and under the earth, when His Holy Name is proclaimed.* People who have disrespectfully used "Jesus" or "God" as a swear word, casually or in vain will fall down in terror on that awesome day. Did you know that what we say about Father God is how we worship Him? Notice the scripture verse in three Bible versions for Exodus 20:7, for total clarity:

"You shall not take the Name of The Lord your God in vain, for The Lord will hold him guiltless who takes his name in vain."

New Living Translation (NLT)

⁷ "You must not misuse the name of the LORD your God. The LORD will not let you go unpunished if you misuse his name.

Amplified Bible (AMP)

⁷You shall not use or repeat the name of the Lord your God in vain [that is, lightly or frivolously, in false affirmations or profanely]; for the Lord will not hold him guiltless who takes His name in vain.

To take the Lord's Name in vain simply means to use His Name in a manner that is not reverent nor with holy respect. The phrase, "the Lord's Name" includes the words, "God," "Jesus," and "Christ." These Holy Names are never, ever to used in any form of exclamation, swearing, or even just what may be considered as casual conversation, such as saying "Oh my ****," which is said all the time in today's society, which flippantly dishonors and trivializes Him.

We do not have the right to exercise authority over God by calling Him out of His Name. The copyright, trademark, patent and all authority of His Name belong exclusively to Him alone. Therefore, He allows us, according to our relationship with Him to use His Name only under certain honorable conditions. Those who love Him show that in their reverent use of His Holy Name, for as Matthew 6:9 teaches us:

"Hallowed [Holy, Respected, Revered, Honored] be Your Name."

Another way that Father God's Name is taken in vain, or dishonored, is through false promises, or making vows, based on Matthew 5:33-35: *"Again you have heard that it was said to those of old, 'You shall not swear falsely, but shall perform to the Lord what you have sworn.' But I say to you, Do not take an oath at all, either by heaven, for it is the throne of God, or by the earth, for it is His footstool, or by Jerusalem, for it is the city of the great King."*

Matthew 5:33-35 New Living Translation (NLT)

³³ *"You have also heard that our ancestors were told, 'You must not break your vows; you must carry out the vows you make to the* LORD*.'* [a] ³⁴ *But I say, do not make any vows! Do not say, 'By heaven!' because heaven is God's throne.* ³⁵ *And do not say, 'By the earth!' because the earth is His footstool. And do not say, 'By Jerusalem!' for Jerusalem is the city of the great King.*

A third way that Father God's Name is taken in vain, or dishonored, is through false prophecies, or making unverified predictions, like the unwise people who predict the timing of the end of the world. These people are imposing on others things that Father God Himself never said, and these statements harm the very people Father God loves. They should stop making stuff up. Listen to the words of Jeremiah 14:14: *"And the Lord said to me: "The prophets are prophesying lies in my name. I did not send them, nor did I command them or speak to them. They are prophesying to you a lying vision, worthless divination, and the deceit of their own minds."*

New Living Translation (NLT)

¹⁴ *Then the* LORD *said, "These prophets are telling lies in my name. I did not send them or tell them to speak. I did not give them any messages. They prophesy of visions and revelations they have never seen or heard. They speak foolishness made up in their own lying hearts.*

The fourth way that people misuse and disrespect Father God's Name is by using His Name for their own benefit, taking the Lord's Name in vain through false pretenses. False pretenses are occasions on which we are pretending to be one of God's people when we are not. Instead, these people are pimping Father God by wanting to be one of His peeps (people) because it beneficial. They want all the benefits, but they don't want any of the commitments. I worked in the hood for many years and in the hood (neighborhood), this would be called "perpetrating," pretending to be what they are not." Or as The Platters, one of my favorite groups from back in the day, used to sing,

Great Pretender

Song by The Platters

Oh-oh, yes I'm the great pretender
Pretending that I'm doing well
My need is such I pretend too much
I'm lonely but no one can tell

Oh-oh, yes I'm the great pretender
Adrift in a world of my own
I've played the game but to my real shame
You've left me to grieve all alone
Too real is this feeling of make-believe
Too real when I feel what my heart can't conceal

Yes I'm the great pretender
Just laughin' and gay like a clown
I seem to be what I'm not, you see
I'm wearing my heart like a crown
Pretending that you're still around

Notice the advice of Matthew 7:21-23 about God's true disciples: *"Not everyone who says to me, 'Lord, Lord,' will enter the kingdom of heaven, but the one who does the will of my Father who is in heaven. On that day many will say to me, 'Lord, Lord, did we not prophesy in your name, and cast out demons in your name, and do many mighty works in your name?' And then will I declare to them, 'I never knew you; depart from me, you workers of lawlessness.'"*

New Living Translation (NLT)

[21] *"Not everyone who calls out to me, 'Lord! Lord!' will enter the Kingdom of Heaven. Only those who actually do the will of my Father in heaven will enter.* [22] *On judgment day many will say to me, 'Lord! Lord! We prophesied in your name and cast out demons in your name and performed many miracles in your name.'* [23] *But I will reply, 'I never knew you. Get away from me, you who break God's laws.'*

Finally, the fifth way that people often take the Lord's name in vain is by making false platitudes, clichés or trite remarks with His Name, which are banned based on Leviticus 19:12: *"You shall not swear by my name falsely, and so profane the name of your God: I am the Lord."* The word "profane" means that our heavenly Father God, The God of the Bible, is The God of Holiness and Ultimate Glory. He is Almighty. He is Worthy of all Praise and Honor. He is to be revered. He is Omniscient and Omnipresent. He is the Reason that the earth, the universe and all we know exist. He is the Reason that we exist. He is the Beginning and The End, The Alpha and Omega. Without Him there is no life. That said, to profane His Holy Name is to use profanity with His Name, which is what is done when we treat Him lightly and inconsequentially, and just dismiss Him. Using the aforementioned examples of commonly used phrases is to make sport of The One True God and make fun of Him. We are to avoid all abuse and disrespect of God's Holy Name. Therefore, let us all resolve from this day forward to only use Father God's Name in ways that honor, revere, respect and worship The Lord.

Therefore, all those who have chosen to draw near to The Lord through obediently following Him in service, adoration and trustingly uttering His Name will be filled with *inexpressible and glorious Joy*. This is our great hope, as we await His glorious return.

For our struggle is not against flesh and blood, but against the rulers, against the authorities, against the powers of this dark world and against the spiritual forces of evil in the heavenly realms. Ephesians 6:12

Therefore God exalted him to the highest place and gave him the name that is above every name, that at the name of Jesus every knee should bow, in heaven and on earth and under the earth. Philippians 2:9-10

Though you have not seen him, you love him; and even though you do not see him now, you believe in him and are filled with an inexpressible and glorious joy, for you are receiving the goal of your faith, the salvation of your souls. 1 Peter1:8–9

And let us not grow weary of doing good, for in due season we will reap, if we do not give up. Galatians 6:9

Selah. By this, I mean, to stop and think on this. For those who do not understand the word selah, here is an explanation of this revered Biblical word and its uses.

According to Wikipedia, Selah (/ˈsiːlə/; Hebrew: סֶלָה, also transliterated as selāh) is a word used seventy-four times in the Hebrew Bible, seventy-one times in the Psalms and three times in Habakkuk. The meaning of the word is not known, though various interpretations are given below. (It should not be confused with the Hebrew word selaʻ (Hebrew: סֶלַע) which means "rock".) It is probably either a liturgico-musical mark or an instruction on the reading of the text, something like "stop and listen." Selah can also be used to indicate that there is to be a musical interlude at that point in the Psalm.[1] The Amplified Bible translates selah as "pause, and think of that." It can also be interpreted as a form of underlining in preparation for the next paragraph.

The Psalms were sung accompanied by musical instruments and there are references to this in many chapters. Thirty-one of the thirty-nine psalms with the caption "To the choir-master" include the word selah. Selah notes a break in the song and as such is similar in purpose to Amen in that it stresses the importance of the preceding passage. Alternatively, selah may mean "forever," as it does in some places in the liturgy (notably the second to last blessing of the Amidah). Another interpretation claims that **selah comes from the primary Hebrew root word salah (סָלָה) which means "to hang," and by implication to measure (weigh).**[2]

Another meaning is given by assigning it to the root, as an imperative that should not properly have been vocalized, "Sollah" (Ewald, "Kritische Grammatik der Hebräischen Sprache,"p. 554; König, "Historisch-Kritisches Lehrgebäude der Hebräischen Sprache," ii., part i., p. 539). The meaning of this imperative is given as "Lift up," equivalent to "loud" or "fortissimo," a direction to the accompanying musicians to break in at the place marked with crash of cymbals and blare of trumpets, the orchestra playing an interlude while the singers' voices were hushed. The effect, as far as the singer was concerned, was to mark a pause. This significance, too, has been read into the expression or sign, selah being held to be a variant of "shelah" (="pause"). But as the interchange of shin ש andsamek ס is not usual in Biblical Hebrew, and as the meaning "pause" is not held to be applicable in the middle of a verse, or where a pause would interrupt the sequence of thought, this proposition has met with little favor. Though there are not any official cases of evidence to support this claim, it is reported in various cities **in the Middle East, that the word selah originates in Syrian Aramaic as a word reserved for prayer as a praise that is used exclusively for praising God and is the highest form of praise man is able to give.** Personally, I am totally in agreement with this final statement, from Wikipedia. By my use of the word selah, I am honoring and praising The Lord, in addition to asking you, dear reader, to think about, or reflect upon, what was just stated in the hopes that you will apply it to your life.

What do you do in the eye of the storm?

In training new teachers, there have been many occasions when the order of the day was a need for encouragement, prayer and hope in the midst of experiencing so many bad things happening at once. So many have shared the following with me, for there have been setbacks in either getting a job, losing a job or difficulties with a current job; fighting with a spouse or significant other; severe illnesses and deaths of close loved ones and friends; sudden distresses with their car working properly; losing a home; severe power outages, wondering what to do for days without any power. Often the question asked was, "Why, God, why?" as the wonderings began to pour out: What did I do to deserve this? Why are you doing this to me? How is all this bad going to turn out for my good?" I have even heard fierce expressions of anger with God as one person shared as we prayed, "I know that even things that seem bad are for my good. Still, I don't know how Not to be angry with You, Lord. Help me, please help me to see this situation with the clarity that will help me get past all this anger so I can feel loving towards You again. Lord, I really miss the closeness that I used to feel with You. Please help me regain it."

In Romans 8:28, Father God's Holy Word says, *And we know that for those who love God all things work together for good, for those who are called according to His purpose.*

When reality and life storms hit us hard, right upside our heads, leaving us reeling from the impact, we cannot help but feel angry, betrayed or even baffled with The Lord. As as result of this anger, we feel ourselves moving away from Him and feeling abandoned. Truthfully, we forget that He never left us, it was us who abandoned Him. This causes us to feel even more disgruntled with ourselves and angrier in the process.

This is one of the most difficult parts of our relationship with Father God to navigate. Did you know that when you feel anger with one another, you need to forgive the one who wronged you? Just stop and forgive: forgive the other person, forgive yourself and forgive your limited perception of the whole matter. Although forgiveness is not the easiest thing to do, it is straightforward and the most necessary.

First, realize that our Heavenly Father God NEVER does us wrong, so there is nothing to forgive Him for. Look to Him and He will calm your storm, enabling you to weather it triumphantly. He is always there for us and with us.

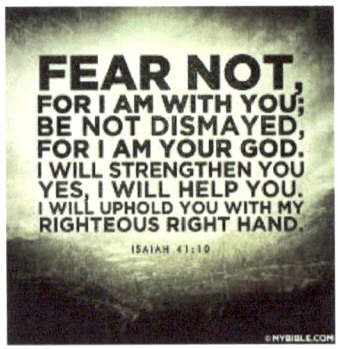

Romans 8:31 Amplified Bible (AMP)

³¹ What then shall we say to [all] this? If God is for us, who [can be] against us? [Who can be our foe, if God is on our side?]

All that anger we tend to feel is the result of our very limited human understanding of how things work in our world and in the spiritual realm. If only we could see through our Father God's eyes, we would never be angry. Just imagine throwing a stone into a still pond of water. Imagine the ripples radiating outwards from that impact. Now, in your mind's eye, see another stone hit and ripple, and another, and still another. Now, try adding a lake surface to that pond and imagine that it runs vertically and intersects with that first pond surface. To that, add in a diagonal lake surface, then add another. Can you imagine all those smooth surfaces intersecting each other? Now imagine 5 billion stones hitting all of these intersecting surfaces and planes, creating ripples that all run into one another. Whew! My head is hurting and surely yours must be too, yes? Yet this is necessary in order to try to understand the multifaceted complexity with which our Heavenly Father God sees things. So when you realize how limited your perception is compared with that of Our Father God, you see how it is best to simply let go of that false perception that He is punishing you, because He is Not punishing you and He Never will.

That is the job and evil intent of our adversary, Satan, who is always concocting evil schemes against Christians to steal, kill and destroy their Godly inheritance. Did you know that it is one of Satan's biggest lies, (after all, he is the father of all lies), that he tells the children of Father God, as a weapon to discourage them and distance them from our Father God, that even if Father God isn't "angry" with them, he wants them to feel in some way, that they have failed Him and now He isn't as thrilled about them as He once was? However, Father God's Word tells us how His heart loves all people, particularly those who choose to love Him and those who repent and turn back to Him. If you question God's heart towards the truly repentant person, then I suggest that you read the entire chapter of Luke 15, where Jesus uses a parable of the lost sheep, the lost coin, and the prodigal son, to illustrate the heart of the Father towards those who return to Him. Although I highly recommend reading the entire chapter, here are a few verses in Luke 15 I want to point out:

Amplified Bible (AMP) A portion of the parable of the prodigal son:

[20] *So he got up and came to his [own] father. But while he was still a long way off, his father saw him and was moved with pity and tenderness [for him]; and he ran and embraced him and kissed him [[a]fervently].*

[21] *And the son said to him, Father, I have sinned against heaven and in your sight; I am no longer worthy to be called your son [I no longer deserve to be recognized as a son of yours]!*

[22] *But the father said to his bond servants, Bring quickly the best robe (the festive robe of honor) and put it on him; and give him a ring for his hand and sandals for his feet.*

[23] *And bring out [b]that [wheat-]fattened calf and kill it; and let us [c]revel andfeast and be happy and make merry,*

^{24} *Because this my son was dead and is alive again; he was lost and is found! And they began to* $^{[d]}$*revel and feast and make merry.*

Know with a firm assurance that Father God's Word confirms His loving kindness and mercy towards all those who turn to Him, and to those who respect and honor Him as noted here in His Word:

Psalm 103:8 Amplified Bible (AMP)

^{8} The Lord is merciful and gracious, slow to anger and plenteous in mercy and loving-kindness.

Psalm 145:8 Amplified Bible (AMP)

^{8} The Lord is gracious and full of compassion, slow to anger and abounding in mercy and loving-kindness.

This proves that Father God is Not a cruel nor a distant taskmaster, as some people believe, because they feel, for example, that He allowed His people, the Israelites, to experience heavy oppression and slavery. This is a perfect example of not considering Father God's side of the story, wherein the Israelites were some of the most rebellious people noted in scripture, for they were even slaughtering their own children to false gods and demons in Psalms 106:37-39:

Amplified Bible (AMP)

^{37} Yes, they sacrificed their sons and their daughters to demons

^{38} And shed innocent blood, even the blood of their sons and of their daughters, whom they sacrificed to the idols of Canaan; and the land was polluted with their blood.

^{39} Thus were they defiled by their own works, and they played the harlot and practiced idolatry with their own deeds [of idolatrous rites].

Trust Father God in the Storms of Life, He Will Bring You Safely Through!

So, know for a fact that when tough times come and trials persist in your life, Father God is Not punishing you and He Never will! Instead, realize the truth that Satan comes to steal, kill and destroy (John 10:10). Once a person feels distant from Father God, for some reason or another, their interests are often directed elsewhere <u>because they are discouraged in their relationship with Father God</u>. This often leads to depression, addictions, obsessions like crafts, movies, sex, sports, and so on, in addition to spending binges and unbalanced life priorities. After a while, the person loses more and more interest in their relationship with Father God, until they simply don't even bother to pick up their Bibles, go to church and spend time with Him. This is how Satan uses discouragement to destroy a person's relationship with our Heavenly Father God. Why?

The whole reason that Satan, who works through evil spirits, wants us to feel discouraged is because he wants to get us to a place where we will just give up. He wants our lovely relationship with Father God to just seem impossible and too hard to maintain. This leads a person to lukewarm relationship with Him and deflates their faith in Father God, because they have no more confidence in their relationship with Him. Herein is the remedy, for the Holy Bible tells us in Hebrews 10:22 to draw near to Father God with all assurance, having our heart's sprinkled clean from an evil conscience, remembering that He has given us the Gift of Eternal Life:

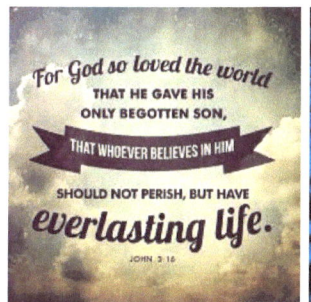 

So let us heed the advice of Hebrews 10:22: *Let us draw near (to God) with a true heart, with full assurance of faith, having our hearts sprinkled from an evil conscience and bodies washed with pure water.* Our adversary, the Devil, the father of all lies, tries to attack us with guilt and shame in order to destroy our confidence in our relationship with Father God Who loves us so much that He gave His life for us on the cross, as noted in John 3:16:

Therefore, realize how limited your perception is compared with that of our loving Heavenly Father God. Let go of any false conviction that our Father God is punishing you. Let me clearly restate the fact that He is Not punishing you and He Never Ever will. Let go of your anger. Take all of our Father God's Goodness on faith for the sake of your soul and your lasting joy as you trust Him in the eye of the storms of life. He will bring you these tough times better, sweeter and stronger, full of joy in Him.

21 Things to Safeguard

Now, please be aware of the 21 things the enemy wants to steal from all who trust, love and believe in Jesus Christ, for John 10:10 says "The thief comes only to steal and kill and destroy." In the life of every Christian, here are 21 vital things the devil targets intentionally and is completely determined to rob us believers of. So, watch, fight and pray for according to I Peter 5:8: *Be sober, be vigilant; because your adversary, the devil, walks about* **like a roaring lion**, **seeking** *whom he may devour. (Have a sober spirit, stay alert for Your adversary, the devil, prowls around* **like a roaring lion**, **seeking** *someone to devour.*

1. **Your Purpose:** It is Divine Purpose that gives a life definition and meaning. A life with no purpose becomes worthless.

2. **Your Desire:** The Holy Bible says that the desires of our hearts shall be granted but when desires are killed, frustration sets in.

3. **Your Vision:** Vision takes a person to their destination. Vision creates room for the next level and enlarges your horizon of influence. When your vision is killed, stagnancy prevails.

4. **Your gifts:** The gifts of a man shall make a way for him and cause him to stand before great men says the word of God. Many have not been able to stand before great men because the gifts which will open this door unto them have been buried.

5. **The fruit of your body:** The devil's desire for your children and children's children is to destroy them. He is after the wasting of your generation and its non-existence.

6. **The fruit of your labour:** The great delight of the devil is profitless hard work. He delights in men and women not having anything to show for their labour.

7. **Your Marriage:** Marriages crash daily at an alarming rate. Once the family unit is broken, the society and nation will have a problem of unity.

8. **Your Calling:** As the kingdom of light threatens the kingdom of darkness, the devil does not want anyone to fulfill their ministry. The fulfillment of your ministry to the devil means the defeat of his own kingdom.

9. **Your Potential:** Potential is defined as what you can do but have not done. The devil prefers it when men and women do not wake up to their own potentials. Ignorance of what you can do leads to an unfulfilled life.

10. **The instrument of your blessing:** When the devil takes this away from you, while others are boldly speaking of The Lord's goodness, you will not have a testimony to share.

11. **Your expectation:** The expectation of many has been killed due to a lack of faith. When you are not expectant of God's manifestations of blessings, you end up receiving nothing.

12. **Your star:** A shining star signifies a colorful destiny. When the devil dims the light of your star, the end result is a wasted life.

13. **Your voice:** Every man has been given a voice by God. One of the joys of the enemy is to silence voices and make sure the authority of your voice is lost.

14. **Your life:** This represents your divine assignment in life. It's the devil's delight when men and women do not discover, start or complete the agenda of God for their lives.

15. **Your Divine Helper:** Divine helpers are those who Father God has raised up to assist you. When the devil rages, he makes sure you miss your Divine Helpers.

16. **Your career:** This symbolizes what you are able to do. When a career is under the attack of the devil, it will struggle to succeed.

17. **You name:** The devil also enjoys erasing the names of families, men, women, children and anyone from existence when they constitute a threat to his dark kingdom.

18. **Your destiny:** Destiny is summed up as your mission here on earth. When a destiny is killed, a man or woman becomes a walking corpse.

19. **The Promises of Father God:** When the devil attacks the Promises of Father God for you, they will not come to pass. The danger of this is that one will remain in the Valley of Promises, instead of arriving at the Mountain Top of Fulfillment.

20. **Your Future:** As Christians, our future is in heaven. Any one who ends up in hell has simply been cheated and outsmarted by the devil.

21. **Your present life:** The devil does not want anyone to complete the number of their days on earth to complete their Divine Mission and Divine Purpose. **Therefore, untimely death is one of the weapons of the devil to fulfill this aim.**

Jesus Christ reminds us in John 10:10 that "I have come that they may have life, and have it to the full." Therefore, the Ministry of Jesus Christ, our Blessed Redeemer, is to undo the works of darkness committed by our evil adversary and his minions. In Christ alone is found deliverance, healing, hope, joy, fulfillment and restoration. Therefore, let us resolved to be filled with Jesus Christ, the Son of Father God. Furthermore, let us resolve to live life to the full by faith with His Help, Guidance, Power, Presence, Ministry, Anointing and Assurance.

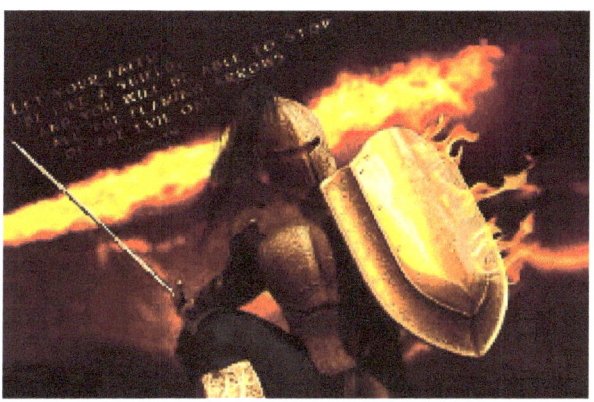

Being Dressed for Battle: Armed and Dangerous

Being Dressed for Battle is critical to living the Christian life, for we do not wrestle against flesh and blood, but we wrestle against spiritual rulers, authorities, powers of this dark world and the spiritual forces of evil. The enemy sees you as armed and dangerous when we are well equipped in the Power of the Name, Word and Blood of God. There are also battles within ourselves, our thought life which we must control daily. So get dressed and have all of your spiritual clothes on.

THE WHOLE ARMOR OF GOD
EPHESIANS 6:10-20

FINALLY, MY BRETHREN, BE STRONG IN THE LORD AND IN THE POWER OF HIS MIGHT. PUT ON THE WHOLE ARMOR OF GOD, THAT YOU MAY BE ABLE TO STAND AGAINST THE WILES OF THE DEVIL. FOR WE DO NOT WRESTLE AGAINST FLESH AND BLOOD, BUT AGAINST PRINCIPALITIES, AGAINST POWERS, AGAINST THE RULERS OF THE DARKNESS OF THIS AGE, AGAINST SPIRITUAL HOSTS OF WICKEDNESS IN THE HEAVENLY PLACES. THEREFORE TAKE UP THE WHOLE ARMOR OF GOD, THAT YOU MAY BE ABLE TO WITHSTAND IN THE EVIL DAY, AND HAVING DONE ALL, TO STAND.

STAND THEREFORE, HAVING GIRDED YOUR WAIST WITH TRUTH, HAVING PUT ON THE BREASTPLATE OF RIGHTEOUSNESS, AND HAVING SHOD YOUR FEET WITH THE PREPARATION OF THE GOSPEL OF PEACE; ABOVE ALL, TAKING THE SHIELD OF FAITH WITH WHICH YOU WILL BE ABLE TO QUENCH ALL THE FIERY DARTS OF THE WICKED ONE. AND TAKE THE HELMET OF SALVATION, AND THE SWORD OF THE SPIRIT, WHICH IS THE WORD OF GOD; PRAYING ALWAYS WITH ALL PRAYER AND SUPPLICATION IN THE SPIRIT, BEING WATCHFUL TO THIS END WITH ALL PERSEVERANCE AND SUPPLICATION FOR ALL THE SAINTS—AND FOR ME, THAT UTTERANCE MAY BE GIVEN TO ME, THAT I MAY OPEN MY MOUTH BOLDLY TO MAKE KNOWN THE MYSTERY OF THE GOSPEL, FOR WHICH I AM AN AMBASSADOR IN CHAINS; THAT IN IT I MAY SPEAK BOLDLY, AS I OUGHT TO SPEAK.

WWW.FREEBIBLESTUDYGUIDES.ORG   2010 DAWN BOOTH

The Armor of God, Our Spiritual Clothing

While all the scriptures in the Holy Bible are meaningful, some of them contain especially deep meanings between the lines for those who know where and how to look. These meanings are generally hidden to those who are unfamiliar or only slightly familiar with the Bible. However, as one becomes better versed in the Scriptures and gains a better understanding of Father God and His plans for our lives, these meanings slowly start to become clear as The Holy Spirit shines down on the reader and reveals these juicy portions of spiritual food to him or her.

One passage containing such a portion of spiritual food is the passage on The Armor of God. This passage, contained in the middle of the sixth chapter of the book of Ephesians, instructs a Christian on how to arm himself or herself for spiritual battle against the forces of Satan, our worst adversary. Fully prepared with the "full armor of God," one can resist the power of the devil and stand triumphant with Jesus Christ when the Spiritual Kingdom of God transcends the line between spiritual and physical, and comes to Earth in physical form. Therefore, let us examine this vital passage right now.

Ephesians 6:10-18 NIV
10 Finally, be strong in the Lord and in His mighty power.
11 Put on the full armor of God so that you can take your stand against the devil's schemes.
12 For our struggle is not against flesh and blood, but against the rulers, against the authorities, against the powers of this dark world and against the spiritual forces of evil in the heavenly realms.
13 Therefore put on the full armor of God, so that when the day of evil comes, you may be able to stand your ground, and after you have done everything, to stand.
14 Stand firm then, with **the belt of truth** *buckled around your waist, with* **the breastplate of righteousness** *in place,*
15 and with **your feet fitted with the readiness that comes from the gospel of peace.**
16 In addition to all this, take up **the shield of faith**, *with which you can extinguish all the flaming arrows of the evil one.*
17 Take **the helmet of salvation** *and* **the sword of the Spirit**, *which is* **The Word of God.**
18 And **pray in the Spirit** *on all occasions with all kinds of prayers and requests. With this in mind, be alert and always keep on praying for all the saints.*

As verse 12 explains, a Christian's battle is against the powers of the nations and the spiritual forces of evil in the heavenly realms. A Christian might believe that he or she can fly 'low under the radar,' sneak quietly by, and pass right by Satan while he is busy attacking some other poor Christian who is uncertain in his or her faith. Unfortunately, it does not work that way. Satan is ever vigilant and watchful, and absolutely will notice each and every mortal man and woman who devotes themselves to Christ.

Each and every new Christian attracts the notice of Satan, and before long, without them even realizing it, they are under spiritual attack. These attacks are subtle and misleading in nature, intended to confuse the Christian so that he or she wanders off the correct path and heads the wrong way, into Satan's realm, often not even knowing that he or she has gone astray. This is why Christians are called sheep and Jesus Christ is called The Shepherd. Jesus, our Shepherd, also becomes our General when we strap on the Armor of God and march into battle against the forces of evil.

Truth, righteousness, the gospel also known as The Word of God, faith, salvation, the spirit, and prayer are a Christian's tools and armaments. They are what enables a Christian to triumph over evil and stand before Father God as a son or daughter worthy of the adoption into Father God's spiritual family. Each tool plays an important part in a Christian's life.

Each tool is also very carefully and properly placed to provide its optimum function. When we read about the "helmet of salvation" in verse 17, it does not become immediately apparent why salvation is the helmet instead of, for example, the footgear or the belt. When a Christian can understand why each piece of the Armor of God is what it is, he or she may wield the full armor to its maximum effectiveness. Let us examine the Armor of God, piece by piece, right now.

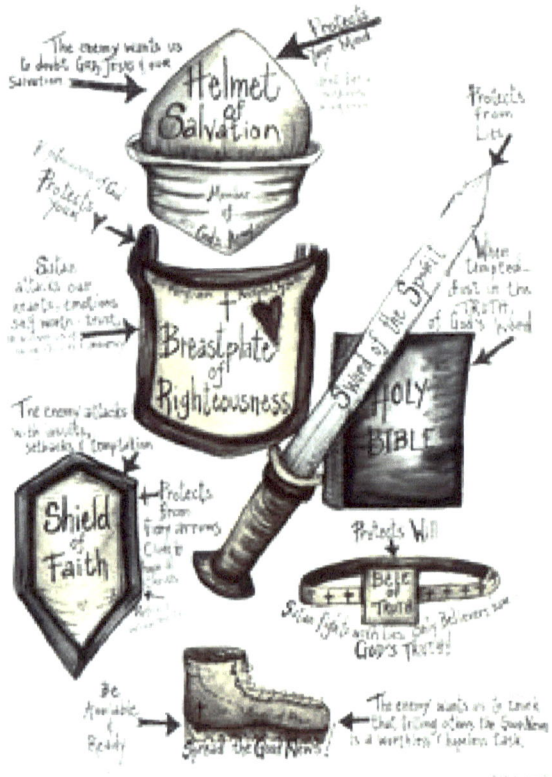

The first piece of the armor is the "belt of truth." In Biblical times, a belt or girdle was what held a person's outfit all together. Robes and tunics were tied at the waist with a belt or girdle. It held the clothing against the body and all in place. So it is with Truth. When a Christian lives, speaks, and breathes truth at all times, this Truth that the Christian lives by, keeps the various facets of his or her life all together and functioning smoothly as a unit. Lies and falsehood make a Christian's life fall apart. Truth keeps it all together.

The second piece of the armor is the "breastplate of righteousness." In ancient times, a breastplate was strapped over the chest to protect the whole front of the torso. Later, breastplates had a plate in back to protect the back as well. This important piece of armor protects one of the most important parts of the body, the heart. Since a Christian's character is measured by what is in his or her heart, it is important to keep the intentions of the heart righteous and holy. This breastplate is akin to a spiritual conscience. If a Christian's heart is righteous, it is shielded from desires and impulses to do unrighteous things. Any time an unrighteous desire or temptation tries to enter a righteous heart, the conscience, or breastplate, keeps it out and insures that the heart stays pure.

Now we come to the "readiness that comes from the Gospel of peace" with which the feet are shod. Soldiers of these times wore greaves on their lower legs to protect them. If a man's legs become too badly injured, he can't stand. If a man can't stand, he can't fight, then he becomes more or less totally helpless in the face of his enemy's onslaught. The Gospel contains Father God's Word. There is a little song, sung in many Churches around the world every Sunday, that goes, "Thy word... is a lamp unto my feet, and a light... unto... my path." The Gospel, when the feet are shod with It or wearing It, lights up the narrow but well marked pathway leading to the Kingdom of God, and makes it easier to walk down that path without wandering off of it.

Next, we have the "shield of faith." A Christian can go far and do things he or she might not normally be able to do, with proper faith. Faith in God, faith in Father God's Son, Jesus Christ, faith in ourselves and in our fellow true Christians is an essential tool in resisting unrighteous temptations and desires. Scriptures abound in the Bible describing what one can accomplish with faith, comparing faith to a shield with which we block out, or ward off, the desire or temptation to do wrong. Shields, in ancient times, were used to block incoming spears, rocks, and arrows. The shield of faith will quench all the "burning arrows of the evil one."

The fifth piece of the armor is the "helmet of salvation." A helmet was worn to protect the head. One solid blow to the head and it could all be over. The head includes the mind, or consciousness, of a person. The helmet of salvation protects and saves the mind, the person's sense of self, from death and brings the mind safely into Father God's Presence.

The sixth piece of the armor is the "sword of the Spirit." The Holy Spirit, the Holy Spirit (or Holy Ghost, from Old English **gast**, "spirit") is the third divine person of the Trinity: the "Triune God" manifested as Father, Son, and Holy Spirit; each person itself being God. The Holy Spirit is compared in The Holy Bible to a double-edged sword that always cuts to the heart of the matter, throughout The Holy Bible. One could not ask for a better tool or weapon with which to smite back the minions of Satan. This is why I am not in favor of the popular use of the word "minions," for like so much of what the media portrays, there is an increasing amount of the evil one's presence by the promotion of his words, images, and representation to lead the unaware astray from Father God, step by step, even causing some to dress, act, speak and think like the evil one's darkness. Be careful who you choose to emulate, for there are eternal consequences.

Finally, we are reminded of the importance of prayer. Prayer, with The Lord's Prayer, an example of how to pray from Matthew 6:9-13 noted below, is our form of communication with Father God. This is the prayer The Lord Jesus Christ taught to His disciples in Luke 11:24 and Matthew 6:9-13. In prayer, Father God is more concerned with our hearts rather than what words we use to pray to Him, for The Lord's Prayer is not a magic formula, rather it is an example or a pattern of how we are to pray. Matthew 6:6-7 explains why:

"But when you pray, go into your room, close the door and pray to your Father, who is unseen. Then your Father, who sees what is done in secret, will reward you. And when you pray, do not use vain repetitions as the heathen do. For they think that they will be heard for their many words."

Therefore when we pray, we are to pour out our hearts to Father God, not simply recite memorized words to God:

Philippians 4:6-7 Amplified Bible (AMP)

[6] Do not fret or have any anxiety about anything, but in every circumstance and in everything, by prayer and petition ([a]definite requests), **with thanksgiving,** *continue to make your wants known to God.*

[7] And God's peace [shall be yours, that [b]tranquil state of a soul assured of its salvation through Christ, and so fearing nothing from God and being content with its earthly lot of whatever sort that is, that peace] which transcends all understanding shall[c]garrison and mount guard over your hearts and minds in Christ Jesus.

Here is how the pattern of prayer breaks down. The words, "Our Father in heaven" teaches us to **Whom** our prayers are addressed to, our heavenly **Father God**. "Hallowed be your name" is telling us to **worship God**, and to **praise Him for who He is**. The phrase "Your kingdom come, Your will be done on earth as it is in heaven" is a reminder to us that we are to **pray for God's plan in our lives and the world, not our own plan**. We are to **pray for God's will to be done, not for our desires**. We are encouraged to **ask God for the things we need** in "give us today our daily bread." "Forgive us our debts, as we also have forgiven our debtors" reminds us to **confess our sins to God and to turn from them, and also to forgive others as God has forgiven us**. In the conclusion of The Lord's Prayer, we see the words, "And lead us not into temptation, but deliver us from the evil one" for this is **a plea for help in achieving victory over sin and a request for protection from the attacks of our adversary, the devil.**

Therefore, The Lord's Prayer is not a prayer that we are to memorize and recite back to Father God, for it is only an example of how we should be praying to Him. Is there anything wrong with memorizing the Lord's Prayer? Of course not! Is there anything wrong with praying The Lord's Prayer back to God? Not if your heart is in it and you truly mean the words you say. Remember, in prayer, God is far more interested in our communicating with Him and speaking from our hearts than He is in the specific words we use, so let us thank Him for His faithfulness, mercy and grace, praise Him for Who He is, worship Him for He is truly worthy, ask for God's will to be done in our lives and in the world we live in, ask Him for what we need, confess our sins to Him, turn from them and ask His forgiveness as we forgive others, ask for help to overcome sin, ask Him for protection from the evil one's attacks and express gratitude for God's gifts and blessings.

Now, as we continue with our discussion of the full armor of Father God, it should be noted that there is one piece of equipment that is deliberately omitted from the passage on the Armor of God. There is no mention of a scabbard or sheath to hold the sword. This is because we must always have **the sword in our hand**, always ready to be wielded, always prepared to use it to smite back the forces of darkness. We do not have time to sheathe the sword and rest, not even for even a little while, nor will we have such a time until the Kingdom of God arrives on Earth.

God, The Master of all known things, is also a true Master-at-Arms. He knows exactly with what to outfit and arm His people so that they can conquer the wicked forces seeking to enslave them.

Matthew 19:17 NIV
17 "Why do you ask me about what is good?" Jesus replied. "There is only One who is good. If you want to enter life, obey the commandments."

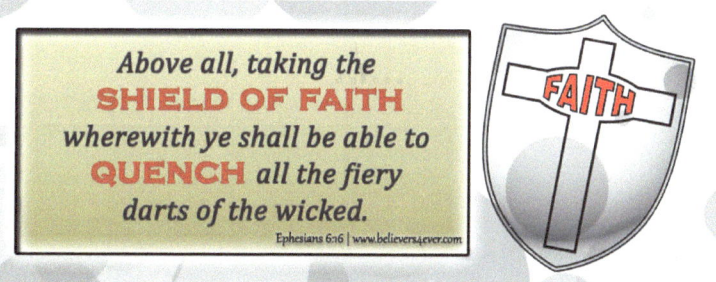

Let's be frank. It is good to know what the armor is and what it is for, yet it is even better to know how to use it. So let's get after it to learn the reasons and the methods for using The Full Armor of God. Notice this vital example of why the armor is necessary in Luke 11:15, 20-22:

14Jesus was driving out a demon that was mute. When the demon left, the man who had been mute spoke, and the crowd was amazed. 15But some of them said, "By Beelzebub,[g] the prince of demons, he is driving out demons." 16Others tested him by asking for a sign from heaven.

17Jesus knew their thoughts and said to them: "Any kingdom divided against itself will be ruined, and a house divided against itself will fall. 18If Satan is divided against himself, how can his kingdom stand?

20But if I drive out demons by the finger of God, then the kingdom of God has come to you.

21"When <u>a strong man, fully armed,</u> guards his own house, his possessions are safe. 22But when someone stronger attacks and overpowers him, he takes away <u>the armor in which the man trusted</u> and divides up the spoils.

Now, that said, let's revisit the passage in Ephesians 6:11-18 to refresh our memories, for any good teacher will tell you that repetition is critically important to build retention of the learned concepts. In the Bible days, men wore tunics, and when it was time to work or do battle, they had to **gird up their loins,** meaning to prepare and strengthen oneself for what is to come, as noted in Jeremiah 1:17-18 and the following illustration: *<u>17</u>"Now, gird up your loins and arise, and speak to them all which I command you. Do not be dismayed before them, or I will dismay you before them. <u>18</u>"Now behold, I have made you today as a fortified city and as a pillar of iron and as walls of bronze against the whole land, to the kings of Judah, to its princes, to its priests and to the people of the land....*

The Armor of God

Ephesians 6:10-18 NIV

10 Finally, be strong in the Lord and in His mighty power.

11 Put on the full armor of God so that you can take your stand against the devil's schemes.

12 For our struggle is not against flesh and blood, but against the rulers, against the authorities, against the powers of this dark world and against the spiritual forces of evil in the heavenly realms.

13 Therefore put on the full armor of God, so that when the day of evil comes, you may be able to stand your ground, and after you have done everything, to stand.

*14 Stand firm then, with **the belt of truth** buckled around your waist, with **the breastplate of righteousness** in place,*

*15 and with **your feet fitted with the readiness that comes from the gospel of peace**.*

*16 In addition to all this, take up **the shield of faith**, with which you can extinguish all the flaming arrows of the evil one.*

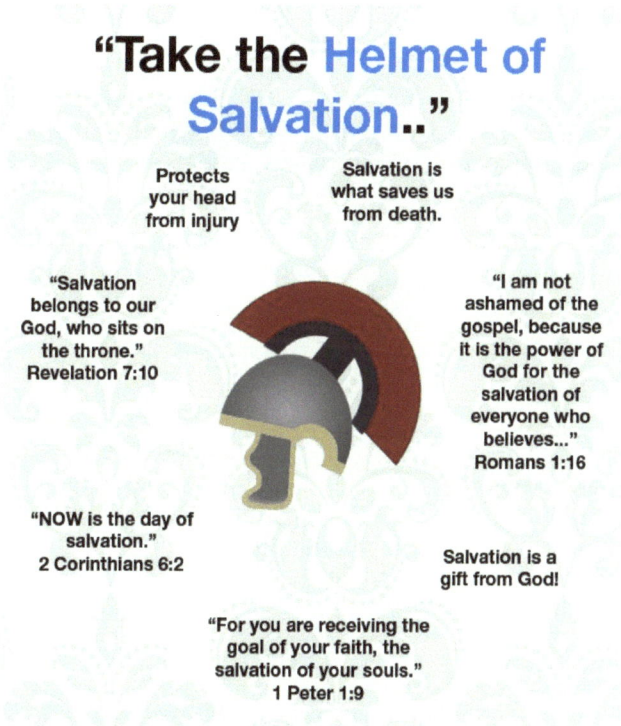

*17 Take **the helmet of salvation** and **the sword of the Spirit**, which is **The Word of God**.*

*18 And **pray in the Spirit** on all occasions with all kinds of prayers and requests. With this in mind, be alert and always keep on praying for all the saints.*

Okay, let me break it down for you, dear reader. *14 Stand therefore having tightened the **belt of truth...***

This means Study the Word, pray more, and believe the Word of Father God.

Why? Notice the instruction of Acts 12:8

Acts 12:8 Amplified Bible (AMP) *⁸ And the angel said to him, **Tighten your belt and bind on your sandals**. And he did so. And he said to him, **Wrap your outer garment around you and follow me**.*

Bottom line: **Tighten your belt to make a supernatural escape.** Father God can help you deal with all of life's varied issues. The Word of God is your path to victory. In Philippians 3:10 Paul said, *"I am determined to know Him in the Power of His resurrection even while I am in the body."* So study in Father God's Word what you are having a problem with. Look up those scriptures in a concordance or in www.biblegateway.com and the scriptures will calm you down, strengthen you, change your mind and help you overcome whatever you are dealing with. As God's Word says in John 8:32, *"The truth will make you free."*

"Stand firm then, with the Belt of Truth buckled firmly around your waist..."

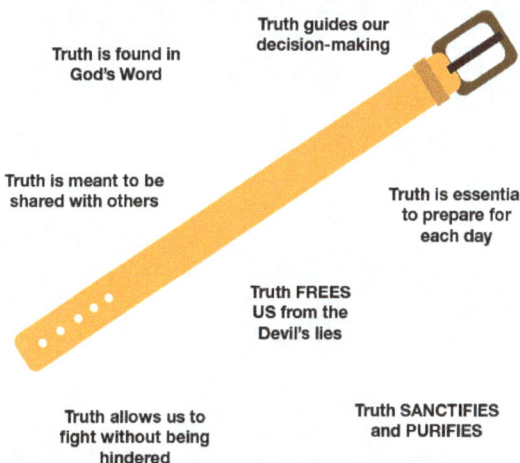

- Truth guides our decision-making
- Truth is found in God's Word
- Truth is meant to be shared with others
- Truth is essential to prepare for each day
- Truth FREES US from the Devil's lies
- Truth allows us to fight without being hindered
- Truth SANCTIFIES and PURIFIES

"With the Breastplate of Righteousness in place."

- Righteousness is something God gives us – we are not righteous on our own
- Righteousness guards against direct attacks on our heart.
- When Jesus has control of our heart, it is protected from attack.
- "Above all else, guard your heart, for it is the wellspring of life." Proverbs 4:23
- "Abraham believed God, and it was credited to him as righteousness." Romans 4:3
- "You have been set free from sin and become slaves to righteousness." Romans 6:18

15 Righteousness: Breastplate of Righteousness

I am the Righteousness of God through Christ.

Know who you are in Christ, according to 2 Corinthians 5:20-21, for we are Ambassadors for Christ and The Righteousness of God in Him:

20Therefore, we are ambassadors for Christ, as though God were making an appeal through us; we beg you on behalf of Christ, be reconciled to God. 21He made Him who knew no sin to be sin on our behalf, so that we might become the righteousness of God in Him.

So work with the Holy Spirit to make the effort to do the right things so Father God can fit you for battle, for He loves you and cares about you. Do not be led by your feelings, for **we walk by faith and not by sight,** as 2 Corinthians 5:7 states.

Remember, Father God always equips you to do what He tells you to do. Live in victory for Revelations 16:15 reminds us:

15"Behold, I come like a thief! Blessed is he who stays awake and keeps his clothes with him, so that he may not go naked and be shamefully exposed."

Recap on the Purpose of The Full Armor of Father God

All Christians are to put on spiritual armour against the enemies of their souls.

Spiritual strength and courage are needed for our spiritual warfare and suffering. Those who would prove themselves to have true grace, must aim at all grace; and put on the whole armor of God, which he prepares and bestows. The Christian armor is made to be worn; and there is no putting off our armor till we have done our warfare, and finished our course. The combat is not against human enemies, nor against our own corrupt nature only, for we have to do battle with an enemy who has a thousand ways of beguiling unstable souls. The devil's assaults intend to rob us of the inheritance that belongs to our souls. The enemy is determined to deface the heavenly image in our hearts. We must resolve by, Father God's grace, guidance and assistance, not to yield to Satan.

Draw Near to God

7Submit therefore to God. **Resist the devil and he will flee from you.** *8Draw near to God and He will draw near to you. Cleanse your hands, you sinners; and purify your hearts…*

If we give way, he will get ground. If we distrust either our cause, or our Leader, Jesus Christ, or our armor, we give the enemy advantage. The different parts of the armor of heavily armed soldiers, who had to sustain the fiercest assaults of the enemy, are described here as:

There is none for the back; nothing to defend those who turn back in the Christian warfare. Truth, or sincerity, is the girdle. This girds on all the other pieces of our armor, and is first mentioned. There can be no relationship with Father God without sincerity. The righteousness of Christ, granted to us, is a breastplate against the arrows of evil wrath. The righteousness of Christ implanted in us, fortifies the heart against the attacks of Satan. Our resolution must be as steadfast as Father God's armor to our legs, enabling us to stand our ground. To march forward in rugged paths, the feet must be shod with the preparation of the gospel of peace. Motives to obedience, amidst trials, must be drawn from a clear knowledge of the Gospel. So studying Father God's Word is critical.

Faith is our all in all in an hour of temptation. Faith, as relying on unseen objects, receiving Christ and the benefits of redemption, and so deriving grace from him, is like a shield, a strong defense every way. The devil is the wicked one. Violent temptations, by which the soul is set on fire straight from hell, are the fiery darts Satan shoots at us. This also includes harsh thoughts of Father God and ourselves to cause us to distrust Him and our faith. Faith requires the daily application of The Word of God and the Grace of Christ to quench the darts of temptation.

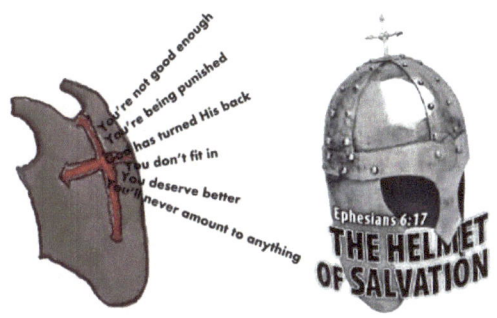

Salvation must be our helmet. A good hope of salvation, a Scriptural expectation of victory, will purify the soul, and keep it from being defiled by Satan. To the Christian armed for defense in battle, the apostle recommends only one weapon of attack; but it is enough, The Sword of the Spirit, which is the Word of God. It subdues and mortifies evil desires and blasphemous thoughts as they rise within, and answers unbelief and error as they assault us from the exterior of our armor. A single Bible text, well understood, and rightly applied, immediately destroys a temptation or an objection, and subdues the most formidable adversary. So commit God's Word to memory, even if only a few short memorized verses at the start.

Prayer must fasten all the other parts of our Christian armor. There are other duties of relationship with The Lord, and of our stations in the world, but we must keep up our times of prayer. Though set and solemn prayer may not be seasonable when other tasks are to be done, yet even short pious prayers make a powerful difference, so do not disregard the power of prayer.

As is often quoted, "The enemy trembles when a Christian's feet or knees hit the floor upon awakening." Prayer is spiritual battle against the unseen evil forces.

We must also use holy thoughts in our daily lives during the course of the day. A vain heart will be vain in prayer. We must pray with all kinds of prayer, public, private, and secret; social and solitary; solemn and sudden: with all the parts of prayer; worship of The Lord, adoration of The Lord, confession of sin, petition for protection from evil, requests that God's Holy Will be done in our lives and on this earth, petition for mercy, and thanksgiving for all divine favor and blessings received. And we must do it all by the grace of God, The Holy Spirit, in dependence on Him, and

according to His teaching. We must pray, not for ourselves only, but for all saints. Our enemies are mighty, and we are without strength, but our Redeemer is Almighty, and in the Power of His might we shall overcome. Therefore we must stir ourselves up and realize that now is the Time for Christ, so let us rise up and fulfill our Divine Purpose. Let us think upon these things, do what we have been instructed by our Lord and General, and continue our prayers with patience.

Ephesians 6:19-24 Amplified Bible (AMP)

[19] And [pray] also for me, that [freedom of] utterance may be given me, that I may open my mouth to proclaim boldly the mystery of the good news (the Gospel),

[20] For which I am an ambassador in a coupling chain [in prison. Pray] that I may declare it boldly and courageously, as I ought to do.

[21] Now that you may know how I am and what I am doing, Tychicus, the beloved brother and faithful minister in the Lord [and His service], will tell you everything.

[22] I have sent him to you for this very purpose, that you may know how we are and that he may [a]console and cheer and encourage and strengthen your hearts.

[23] Peace be to the brethren, and love joined with faith, from God the Father and the Lord Jesus Christ (the Messiah, the Anointed One).

[24] Grace (God's undeserved favor) be with all who love our Lord Jesus Christ with undying *and* incorruptible [love]. *Amen (so let it be).*

What are you made of?

Now, having shared these facts which I pray will help you weather any storm, allow me to share my version of an old anonymous story that has proven during my mentoring of new teachers to be very helpful. May it also inspire and encourage you, dear reader.

One day, a young woman went to visit her mother. She was feeling sad and had no idea how she was going to make her life better. She sat down with her mother and sobbed for a long time while her mother hugged her. The daughter finally stopped crying. As she dried her tears, she told her mother about her life and how everything was just so terribly hard for her. She did not know how she was going to make it. All she wanted to do was give up. She was just so tired of fighting, striving and struggling. It seemed to her that as soon as one problem was solved, a new one came into her life, one right after another. She was so exhausted at the end of talking, that she just leaned back in the chair and wept again.

After listening to her daughter for a while, her wise, loving mother had an idea. Her mother gently took her daughter's hand and led her to the kitchen. The kitchen had always been their favorite room in the house. It was filled with wonderful memories of cooking, laughing, and loving times spent together. The mother filled three of her largest pots with cold water as she quietly hummed a familiar gospel melody. Then she placed each pot on a high fire. Soon, each of the pots came to a boil. In the first pot, Mother placed a group of clean, loose, baby carrots. In the second pot, she placed several medium sized eggs. Finally, in the last large pot, Mother put in some ground coffee beans. She let each pot sit and boil, as she continued to hum, rocking her weary daughter gently in her arms until her daughter was relaxed, without saying a single word.

About twenty minutes later, Mother quietly rose from her chair, allowing her daughter to continue relaxing, and turned off all three of the burners. She took a strainer and three large porcelain bowls out of the cupboard. Then she lifted all of the carrots out of the pot and put them in one of the three bowls. Next, the loving mother removed all of the eggs out of the pot and put them in another bowl. Then she took an old black ladle off the hook where she kept all her cooking utensils. Mother ladled some of the coffee out the pot and into the third large bowl. At last, turning to her beloved daughter, Mother said to her, "Tell me what you see." Her daughter replied, "Well, I see some cooked carrots, some boiled eggs, and some hot coffee."

"Hmmm," was all that Mother replied as she brought her daughter closer to the bowls, and asked her to feel the carrots. The daughter did and she commented that they felt soft and warm. The mother then asked the daughter to take a boiled egg out of the bowl and break it. After pulling off the shell, the daughter observed the white, smooth, hard boiled egg. Finally, the mother asked her daughter to dip a spoon into the bowl and sip some of the coffee. The daughter smiled as she tasted its rich aroma.

The wondering daughter then asked, "What does all this mean, Mother?" "Ah," her mother explained, "Each of these objects faced the same adversity of the boiling water, and each object reacted differently."

"The carrot went in strong, hard and unrelenting. However, after being subjected to the boiling water for a period of time, the carrot softened and became weak."

"The egg had been fragile from the start. Its thin outer shell had protected its liquid interior, but after sitting in the boiling water, the egg's insides hardened."

"However, the ground coffee beans were uniquely different. After they were in the boiling water for a period of time, the coffee beans changed the water into coffee. "Now, which one are you?" the wise mother asked her daughter. "When adversity knocks on your door, how do you respond? Are you more like a carrot, an egg, or a coffee bean?" 'I get it!" exclaimed the smiling daughter. Joyfully, she thanked and hugged her mother for sharing this amazing gift of teaching her such powerful lessons of wisdom through cooking.

Now it is your turn to think about this lesson and apply it to your life. Ask yourself the following questions: Which food am I most like? Am I the carrot that seems strong? In pain and adversity, do I wilt, become soft and lose my strength?

Am I like the egg that starts with a good heart, but changes with the enduring heat? Did I have a fluid, available spirit, but after a death, a breakup, a financial hardship or some other trial, have I become hardened and stiff? Does my outer shell look the same? On the inside, have I become bitter, unyielding and tough with a stiff spirit and hardened heart, refusing to change?

Is it possible that I am more like the coffee bean, for the coffee bean actually changes the boiling hot water, the very circumstance that brings the pain? When the water gets hot, the coffee bean releases the fragrance and flavor. May you and I be like the coffee bean in our daily lives. When things are at their worst, may we get better and change the situation for good around us. When the hour is the darkest and the trials are at their greatest, let us choose to inspire and encourage ourselves and others, making life rich and flavorful. How do you handle adversity? Are you a carrot, an egg, or a coffee bean?

Things to Remember:

The brightest future will always be based on a forgotten past; you can't go forward in life until you let go of your past failures and heartaches.

When you were born, you were crying and everyone around you was smiling. Live your life so at the end, you're the one who is smiling and everyone around you is crying.

May you have enough happiness to make you sweet, enough trials to make you strong, enough sorrow to keep you human and enough hope to make you happy. – Aurora A. Ambrose

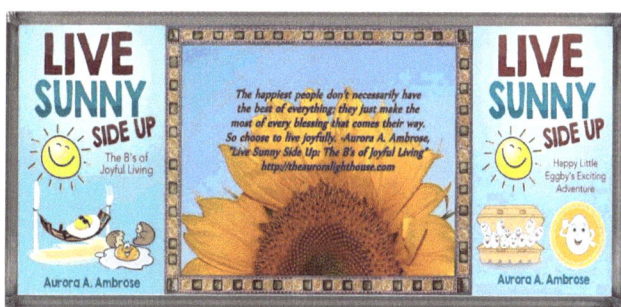

Triumphantly Overcoming a Crushed Spirit

Where do we go and what do we do when negativity, death, divorce, despondency, depression and countless other debilitating life experiences cause us to forget how to live sunny side up? Proverbs 18:14 tells us, "A man's spirit sustains him in sickness, but a crushed spirit who can bear?" Or in the Living Bible it says, "What hope is left?"

In order to bounce back from life's difficulties, we need to assess where we are and where we need to go. In every area of our lives, during the good and the bad times, we need to make daily deposits of success. In the good times, these deposits keep us buoyant. In the bad times, these same deposits help us survive and begin to see there is hope. Even taking tiny withdrawals during tough times without making any replacement deposits will lead to bankruptcy in our relationships, our health, as well as in our jobs and finances. I know that when we are in crisis, the area of the most pain gets most of our attention. Often, it is by making extra deposits in other areas that a person can springboard back to success in even the most critical ones. How can this be accomplished? Here are a few suggestions and Godly affirmations:

- Set aside time for vigorous physical exercise. Walk at least two to three miles every day. This will help energize you, wash away anger and stimulate positive creativity. Smile while you walk and notice all birds, trees, flowers, the sky and even the children. Notice the beauty all around you and give thanks.

- Seek out a godly mentor. Much of the success of Alcoholics Anonymous has been in having another person to call in the lowest times. Never isolate yourself. Maintain strong family and friend relationships. Remember, there is strength in numbers.

- Reduce TV watching and instead read or listen to inspirational material at least two hours daily.

- Volunteer for a worthy cause. Helping someone else in need is a great way to ease the inward pain.

- Forgive everyone in your life. Make peace with your past. Life is too short to waste time hating anyone.

- Get a job – even if it's not your dream job or a great career move. Deliver pizzas or work in the garden department at Home Depot to get moving in a positive direction while you continue to build for long-term success. Yesterday's Nashville Tennessean lists 1814 jobs – and we know that listed jobs represent only about 12% of what's available at any given time; thus there are more than 15,000 positions waiting to be filled in this average sized city.

- At the end of each day, complete these two sentences:

  "Today I am thankful for......"

  "Today my most significant accomplishment was......."

I recognize that some losses are irretrievable and an overload of pain is debilitating. If you recognize multiple withdrawals in your life, take drastic measures to stop the hemorrhaging and start making deposits in the areas you can control today! Let these Godly affirmations assist you.

Let these Godly affirmations assist you.

- I am the righteousness of God.
- I receive the blessings of God.
- God abundantly supplies all of my needs.
- God loves me unconditionally.
- Being positive does not mean I deny the difficulties in life, it means I believe that God is greater than my difficulties.
- Optimism is contagious, so I choose to bring positive, Godly divine connections into my life.
- I do not have to meditate on just anything that pops into my head. I can choose my own positive thoughts.
- God has a great purpose for my life and He causes me to triumph and succeed in whatever He directs me to do.
- I believe that I will experience greater intimacy with my heavenly Father than ever before.
- I believe that I will experience a new beginning in God.
- My job is to stop allowing myself to get frustrated and upset.
- I am going to zip my lip when God prompts me to.
- I will have peace with people.
- I forgive quickly.

- I will never say anything negative about myself again.
- God didn't make any junk.
- I believe that every yoke of sickness, depression, anxiety, financial trouble, family problems and more will be broken in my life.
- I believe that I will be productive in the image of Christ.
- I believe that I will come out of my trials and challenges ready and positioned for God's greatness.
- I believe that I will discover the call of God on my life and learn how I fit into His divine plan.
- I believe that my family, friends, and others will see salvation because of the light in my life.
- I believe that I will experience greater intimacy with my heavenly Father than ever before.
- I believe that I will begin walking in my perfect purpose and destiny that God created for me.
- I am blessed coming in and going out.
- My family and I find favor with our bosses and our teachers.

More *Jesus* Less Drama
Less Selfishness
Less Complaining
Less Bitterness
Less Gossip
Less Pride
Less Anger
Less Me

- I will not easily offended.
- I believe the best of people.
- I call the things that are not as though they are.
- I will get myself in agreement with God.
- I can do all things through Christ who strengthens me.
- The joy of the Lord is my strength.
- I will not complain because when I do I am not trusting God.
- I can be pitiful or powerful, but I cannot be both. I choose powerful.
- I trust God completely, so I do not worry.

- I shall lend and not borrow.
- This is the day of the Lord. I will enjoy my day.
- I am putting on my righteousness.
- I am putting on my peace.
- I am going to use the Sword of the Spirit, God's Word, daily.
- I am going to lift up the shield of faith.
- I am going to put on love.
- I am going to put on the helmet of salvation.
- I am going to get spiritually dressed today.
- I am going to put on mercy.
- God is my manna.
- Jesus is the bread of life that I need now.
- I am going to be a peacemaker and maintainer of peace today.
- If I do not get my way, I will just adapt and be happy anyways.
- I will be mindful to be a blessing to everyone today.
- I will complement every person that needs encouraging today.
- I will not live my life in bondage.
- If anyone can be free it will be me.
- Being positive does not mean I deny the difficulties in life, it means I believe that God is greater than my difficulties.
- God teach me something valuable as I press through the situation at hand.
- I will choose to look for the good out of every negative, bad situation. There is always something to learn.
- Help me to let my emotions subside before I make important decisions.
- I do not make my decisions based on my feelings.
- I will overcome evil with good. Romans 12:21
- Always being right is highly overrated.
- Help me not to let others limited thinking, limit me.

- I shall possess a double portion of what I have forfeited, and I shall receive it in this life time, according to Isaiah 61:7:
- Instead of your shame you will receive a double portion, and instead of disgrace you will rejoice in your inheritance.
- I believe that You, God, are in charge of my life.
- You are my defender and You are my vindicator.

- I know that real promotion comes from God.
- Nobody can keep me from having Your best in my life if I keep my eyes on You.
- I refuse to do anything without the power of God in my life.
- There is no sickness in my house.
- God has pleasure in my prosperity
- I shall run and not grow weary.
- I shall walk and not faint.
- I will wait on the Lord and He will renew my power and strength.
- I will see my dreams come true.

- Lord, make me strong inside that the eyes of my heart might be flooded with light.
- Help me to know the greatness of Your power.
- Help me do all things without complaining Phil 2:14
- Help me to learn to choose and prize what is excellent.
- Help me to choose the highest and the best and be able to discern and know the difference.
- Help me to know what is real and genuine and what is not.
- Help me to take in Your Word, the Bible, not as just head knowledge but to have it sink into my heart so it can be developed in my personality.
- Help me to be a light in this darkened world for Your glory and not my own.
- Help me to know what is of real value and what is not.
- Help me to know Your will and exercise every kind of patience, always giving thanks.
- I pray for my enemies to be blessed.
- Help me to pray before I come into temptation, and not wait until after I have already sinned.
- Help me God to run and not be weary and to walk and not faint or become tired. Isaiah 40:31

- Help me be committed to excellence and to come up higher.
- Help me to know where my part ends and Your part begins.
- Help me to do what I can do, and cast the rest of my care on You, Lord.

- Help me to understand that laboring in the flesh produces no fruit.
- Help me to rest in God and to be seated in Him.
- Help me not to stress about the things that I can do nothing about, but to leave it to God's will.
- Help me receive Your love so I can love others.
- Help me to hold my peace, remain in rest, so You can fight for me.

- God is faithful.
- God will defeat my enemies.
- God is my vindicator.
- I believe God's promise that I am a part of the world wide ministry.
- I have favor in my life.
- I expect to have a strong, long life.
- I do all things unto the Lord.
- I will not be a people pleaser because I care what God thinks of me more than I care what others think.

- Only God is my rock and my salvation.
- God is my defense and my fortress. I shall not be moved. Ps 62:6
- I love myself because God loved me first.
- I have a great personality.
- I am not where I am supposed to be, but thank God I am not where I used to be.
- God has left me his peace, so I have peace in me.
- I am anointed by God.
- I have gifts and talents.
- I have creativity.
- I am a cool person to get to know.
- I am going to stay out of other people's business.
- I will operate in peace today.
- I acknowledge every good thing that is in me.
- Joy and righteousness is in me.
- I am fearfully and wonderfully made.
- I am willing to give up what God is prompting me to give up.
- Help me to be humble.

- Complaining is a bad attitude expressed in grumbling.
- Being blameless does not mean sinless perfection, it means above reproach.
- Help me to become spiritually mature.
- I am in right standing with You God.
- I will not bow down to fear.
- I am able to do whatever I need to do or are lead to do.
- I always have a positive attitude.

- I will be loving even to the unlovely.
- Even my enemies can't help but to bless my life.
- I obey God promptly.
- I do not make decisions based on feelings.
- I am very generous.
- I am careful about what I say to others and say about myself.
- I treat people the way I want to be treated
- Help me to think on something good, because there should be no room for wrong thoughts to stay in my mind and be meditated on continuously.
- I can choose what I want to think about. Help me to choose positive thoughts on purpose.
- Help me to remember to speak positive thoughts out loud, because speaking positive words out loud blocks, cancels out, negative, condemning thoughts.
- I cannot just wait for something positive to fall into my head, but I have to speak positive words on purpose, even when I feel negative.
- My feelings and emotions have nothing to do with my decisions to do the right thing.
- Help me be rooted in love.
- Help me to be filled with the fullness of God and become just a body, wholly filled and flooded with God himself.
- Lord, make me strong inside that the eyes of my heart might be flooded with light.
- Help me to know the greatness of Your power.
- Help me do all things without complaining Phil 2:14
- Help me to learn to choose and prize what is excellent.
- Help me to choose the highest and the best and be able to discern and know the difference.

- Help me to know what is real and genuine and what is not.
- Help me to take in Your Word, the Bible, not as just head knowledge but to have it sink into my heart so it can be developed in my personality.
- Help me to be a light in this darkened world for Your glory and not my own.
- Help me to know what is of real value and what is not.
- Help me to know Your will and exercise every kind of patience, always giving thanks.
- I pray for my enemies to be blessed.
- Help me to pray before I come into temptation, and not wait until after I have already sinned.
- Help me God to run and not be weary and to walk and not faint or become tired. Isaiah 40:31
- Help me be committed to excellence and to come up higher.
- Help me to know where my part ends and Your part begins.
- Help me to do what I can do, and cast the rest of my care on You, Lord.
- Help me to understand that laboring in the flesh produces no fruit.
- Help me to rest in God and to be seated in Him.
- Help me not to stress about the things that I can do nothing about, but to leave it to God's will.
- Help me receive Your love so I can love others.
- Help me to hold my peace, remain in rest, so You can fight for me.
- Thank you, Lord!
- Thank you for Your son dying on the cross for my sins.
- Thank you for Your Tenderness.
- Thank you for my children.
- Thank you for my husband/Wife.
- Thank you for our health.
- Thank you for my life.
- You are my hope.
- Thank you for my strength in You.
- Thank you for Your sense of humor.
- Lord, You are my life.
- You are my hope.

- You are my strength, my song and my salvation. Isaiah 43
- Thank you for Your Kingdom.
- Thank you for your unfailing mercy, grace and truth.
- Thank you for Your faithfulness and honesty.
- Thank you for my faith.
- Thank you for Your Holy Spirit.
- Thank you for my home, my health, my life, my blessings and my freedom.
- Thank you for knowledge, wisdom and understanding of Your Word, the Bible.
- Thank you for my right standing with You.
- Thank you for the forgiveness of my sins.
- Thank You for my salvation, my testimony and eternal life.

The Meaning of the Phrase, Dying to Self

The concept of "dying to self" is found throughout the New Testament. It expresses the true essence of the Christian life, in which we take up our cross and follow Christ. Dying to self is part of being born again; the old self dies and the new self comes to life, according to John 3:3–7. Not only are Christians born again when we come to salvation, but we also continue dying to self as part of the process of sanctification. As such, dying to self is both a one time event and a lifelong process. Jesus spoke repeatedly to His disciples about taking up their cross, for the cross is an instrument of death, and following Him. He made it clear that if any would follow Him, they must deny themselves, which means giving up their lives, particularly their self centeredness, to focus on Him, spiritually, symbolically, and even physically, if necessary. This was a prerequisite for being a follower of Jesus Christ, Who proclaimed that trying to save our earthly lives would result in our losing our lives in the kingdom. Those who would give up their lives for His sake would find eternal life, as verified in Matthew 16:24–25 and Mark 8:34–35. In fact, Jesus even went so far as to say in Luke 14:27 that those who are unwilling to sacrifice their lives for Him *cannot* be His disciples.

The rite of baptism expresses the commitment of the believer to die to the old, sinful way of life, as explained in Romans 6:4–8, and be reborn to a new life in Christ. In Christian baptism, the action of being immersed in the water symbolizes dying and being buried with Christ. The action of coming out of the water pictures Christ's resurrection. Baptism identifies us with Christ in His death and resurrection, **portraying symbolically the whole life of the Christian as a dying to self and living for and in Him who died for us** as noted in Galatians 2:20.

Paul explains to the Galatians the process of dying to self as one in which he has been "crucified with Christ," and now Paul no longer lives, but Christ lives in him. Paul's old life, with its propensity to sin and to follow the ways of the world, is dead, and the new Paul is the dwelling place of Christ who lives in and through him. This does not mean that when we "die to self" we become inactive or insensible, nor do we feel ourselves to be dead. Rather, dying to self means that the things of the old life are put to death, most especially the sinful ways and lifestyles we once engaged in. *"Those who belong to Christ Jesus have crucified the sinful nature with its passions and desires,"* Galatians 5:24. Whereas we once chose to pursue selfish pleasures and self centered goals, instead we now pursue, with equal passion, that which pleases God. This is not something that is immediately accomplished, rather it is a work of The Holy Spirit in each of us as we grow into The Lord's likeness through various life experiences that teach us volumes.

Dying to self is never portrayed in Scripture as something optional in the Christian life since it is the reality of the new birth. No one can come to Christ unless he is willing to see his old life crucified with Christ and begin to live anew in obedience to Him. Jesus describes lukewarm followers who try to live partly in the old life and partly in the new as those whom He will spit out, according to Revelation 3:15–16. This lukewarm condition characterized the church of Laodicea, as well as many churches today. Being "lukewarm" is a symptom of unwillingness to die to self and live for Christ. Death to self is not an option for Christians, rather, it is a choice that leads to fulfillment, a deeper intimacy with our Lord, a meaningful testimony and most of all, eternal life. That said, please allow me to share with you an insightful reading that was given to me by my late beloved grandmother, entitled Dying to Self by an anonymous author, with my personal revisions.

Dying to Self

When you are forgotten, or neglected, or purposely set at naught, and you don't sting and hurt with the insult or the oversight, but your heart is happy, being counted worthy to suffer for Christ…

THAT IS DYING TO SELF

When your good is evil spoken of, when your wishes are crossed, your advice disregarded, your opinions ridiculed, and you refuse to let anger rise in your heart, or even defend yourself, but take in all in patient, loving silence…

THAT IS DYING TO SELF

When you lovingly and patiently bear any disorder, any irregularity, any impunctuality, or any annoyance; when you stand face to face with waste, foolishness, folly, extravagance, spiritual insensibility and endure it as Jesus endured...

THAT IS DYING TO SELF

When you are content with any food, any offering, any climate, any society, any raiment, any interruption by the will of God...

THAT IS DYING TO SELF

When you never care to refer to yourself in conversation, or to record your own good works, or itch after commendations, when you can truly love to be unknown...

THAT IS DYING TO SELF

When you can see your brother prosper and have his needs met and can honestly rejoice with him in spirit and feel no envy, nor question God, while your own needs are far greater and in desperate circumstances...

THAT IS DYING TO SELF

When you can receive correction and reproof from one of less stature than yourself and can humbly submit inwardly as well as outwardly, finding no rebellion or resentment rising up within your heart...

THAT IS DYING TO SELF

Are you dead to yourself yet? In these last days, the Holy Spirit would bring us to the cross...

> *"That I may know Him, and the power of his resurrection, and the fellowship of his sufferings, being made conformable unto his death."* Phil.3:10

WHAT OTHERS MAY DO, YOU MUST NOT DO!

My dearest late friend and prayer partner, Demita Usher, (Oh, how I miss her!) would converse often with me about our many earthly trials. In the course of those discussions, either she or I would ask, "Why me?" or "Why is it so hard on us as believers when we see others who are not what they should?" Well, in response to that I finally realize some pertinent facts. If God has really called us to be like Jesus, He will draw us into a life of crucifixion and humility. As the old hymn says, "Must Jesus bear the cross alone and everyone go free? No, just as there was a cross for Him, there's a cross for you and me." Therefore, He will put upon us such demands of obedience, that we will not be able to follow what other people do, nor measure ourselves by other Christians, and in many ways He will seem to let other people do the very things which He will not let us do.

Other Christians and ministers, who seem very religious and useful, may push themselves, pull wires and work schemes to carry out their plans, but you and I cannot do that. If we attempt to do it, we will meet with such failure and rebuke from the Lord that we will be very regretful and filled with repentance. So let us realize that The Divine Silversmith, Father God, is doing a work in us, so much so, that just like a silversmith, He will continue the firing and polishing process used in making silver until He sees His image in us more clearly.

So, others may boast about themselves, their work, their successes, their plans, and their writings, but the Holy Spirit will not allow you to do any such thing. If you begin to do any of it, He will lead you into deep mortification that will make you despise yourself and all your good works.

Others may be allowed to succeed in making money, or may have a legacy left to them, but it may be God will keep you living within your means while being totally content doing so, because He wants you to have something far better than silver and gold, namely, a helpless dependence upon Him, so that He may have the privilege of supplying your needs daily from an unseen Heavenly Treasury as you walk by faith in Him, not by sight of what you see all around you.

The Lord may let others be honored and put forward, and keep you hidden in obscurity, because He wants to produce in you some choice anointing, a fragrant spiritual fruit for His coming Glory, a fruit of such value which can only be produced in life's shade experiences. He may let others be great, but keep you small and unrecognized, totally incognito. He may let others do a work for Him and get the credit for it, but He will make you work and toil on without knowing how much you are doing; and then to make your work still more precious, He may let others get credit for the work which you have done, and make your reward ten times greater when Jesus Christ comes.

The Holy Spirit will put a strict watch over you, with a jealous love, and will rebuke you for little words and feelings or for wasting your time, which other Christians never feel distressed over. So make up your mind that God is The Infinite Sovereign Lord and He has a right to do as He pleases with His own. He may not explain to you a thousand things which puzzle you, nor explain any of the reasons for His dealings with you. Yet if you absolutely sell yourself to be His and His alone, exclusively, He will wrap you up in a jealous love, and endow you with so many blessings which only come to those who are in His inner circle.

So let us settle it forever, then, that you will commit yourself completely to Jesus Christ as Savior and Lord Almighty, and as such, that He has the right to tie your tongue, or chain your hand, or close your eyes, in ways that He does not seem to use with others. When you are so filled with the Living Almighty God that you are, in your secret heart, pleased and delighted over this peculiar, personal, private, jealous guardianship and management of the Holy Spirit over your life, you will have found the Unmatched Delight and Treasure of Heaven.

Encourage Yourself!

There are times in each of our lives that we may find that we need some encouragement to boost and uplift us when we are dealing with tough times. May the following lyrics, scriptures, thoughts and poetry speak ever so powerfully to your heart, meeting your innermost needs, enabling you to know, grow, show and glow brighter like the noonday sun!

Praise God from Whom All Blessings Flow

1 Praise God, from whom all blessings flow;
   Praise Him, all creatures here below;
   Praise Him above, ye heav'nly host;
   Praise Father, Son, and Holy Ghost!

2 Praise God, the Father Who's the source;
   Praise God, the Son Who is the course;
   Praise God, the Spirit Who's the flow;
   Praise God, our Portion here below!

Lyrics: Thomas Ken, v. 1 (1637-1711)
Music: From Genevan Psalter (1551)
https://www.hymnal.net/en/hymn/h/8

Praise God from Whom All Blessings Flow
My Levitical Poetic Doxology
Aurora A. Ambrose/Vicki Evans

Praise God, from Whom all blessings flow;
Praise Him, all people and living things here below;
Praise Him, all over the earth and all of heaven above
Praise Father God, Jesus Christ the Son, and The blessed Holy Ghost!
Three in One, and One in Three, They are The Blessed Trinity
Praise Father God, Who is Our Help and Source;
Praise Jesus Christ, His Son, Who is Our Course

Praise The Holy Spirit Who is Our Guiding Flow;
Praise Jehovah God, Our Inheritance, for all to know!
When you are born into this glorious life, by God's grace, that is Divine Invitation.
When you encourage others to do great things, that is exhortation.
When you enter a life apart from God and His grace, that's isolation
When you express your love for God, that's adoration
When God comes to see you, that's visitation
When you celebrate God with all honor, that's acclamation
When you encourage others to do great things, that is exhortation.
When He unveils the mysteries of eternity, that's revelation
When you think of His marvelous goodness, that's meditation
When you expect to see Him, that's anticipation
When you work hand in hand with your fellow man, that's cooperation
When you feel God's Spirit moving in your heart, that's motivation
When you share in Kingdom building, that's participation
When you tell of His goodness and His mercy, that's recitation
When you glorify and praise The Lord, that's worship and celebration
When you receive His favor and blessings, that's manifestation
When you await His return and your heavenly reward, that's expectation
When you develop your God-given talents, that's cultivation
When all of these delights are part of your life experience,
And when you've overcome victoriously the worst of life's storms

You can't help but shout Hallelujah and give God His due praise
As you give your testimony, someone else's bowed head you'll raise
As they see the victory is given to the one who endures, not to the swift
And realize that living this life is a precious, divine Gift

Oh you may not do praise The Lord the way others do
But you'll do something, to express just how good He's been to you
When you look around and see all the wonders He has done
Given you breath, life, hope, health and salvation through His Son
Your two eyes you open, your body you can move,
Your brain that thinks, your talents He shows Himself through
The fact that He woke you up and gave you a brand new day
You can't help but be thankful in every single way
He didn't have to do it, but He chose to love you so
That here you are, blessed to be a blessing to those you know
Let go, give vent to the Holy Spirit and let Him overflow
Joyous shouts from your lips, or a tear from your eyes
A clap from your hands, or a stomp of your feet just to let Him know
That you are indeed grateful for all the marvelous blessings on you
He bestows

Something will move within you, something will touch your heart
Causing you to praise God, The Source of All Blessings
Right from the very start

Praise Almighty God
Who spoke to the heavens and created every star, planet and galaxy
Took dust and made man, breathed the breath of life into him
Made a woman from man's rib
And together they lived and ruled the earth
God formed the earth and dressed it in water and green land
Filled it with every living thing that we see, all from His hand
With four legs, two legs, wings, beaks and tails
On earth or in the seas, all were formed by His command
Every animal, plant and tree, all of nature's glory and beauty
Fruits, vegetables, gladiolas, tulips, orchids, roses, daisies and the lily

Praise The Everlasting God
Who established the Counsel of The Holy Trinity
He organized the angelic host who praise Him forever
Providing the music that is the orchestral theme song
To all He Is, Does and Ever Shall Be
While The Glory of our Heavenly Father flooded the City of Bethlehem
Prepared the virgin Mary to conceive
Then He took off His heavenly robes
And entered this earth to be born as a swaddling baby
To teach this world what Real Love is and does
As He chose to sacrifice Himself for each of us
Alone on the cross up on the hill, yes, this He chose
Suffered, beaten, spit on, bled, died and arose
In Resurrection Glory, to sit on the right hand of God the Father
Helping every Believer as they toil and stand the test
Enabling and anointing each one to do their best

Praise Almighty God
Who is my Shelter, Strength and Song
He makes me live like I'm rich
And helps me love like there's no wrong
Praise God, my Rest
Who helps me sleep like a worryless baby
On a pillow of safety and comfort
He opens doors that no man can shut
He provides everything as The Good Shepherd
The sheep have no fear for He is near
They dwell richly in green pastures
Beside the still waters
They hear His voice and follow Him
Ask and you shall receive
Knock on the door, it shall be opened

Praise God
For He is Our Rock, Our Refuge and Our Help
Besides Him, there is no one else
He is Our Strength, Our Hope and Our Guide
He is Our Salvation, Our Life and Our Peace

Praise God

He is Our Lord, Our Savior, Our All in All
Because of Him, we have the Assurance
That we will Live with Him Forever
In that grand celestial home called Heaven
Where there will be no more pain,
No more tears
No more worries
No more fears
There will be only Hello
And never Goodbye
On that blessed shore
Where we'll praise Him
Singing, dancing, Hallelujahs
All the while
Praise God
Praise God
Praise God
From Whom All Blessings Flow
Praise God
Now and Forevermore!

Praise God from Whom All Blessings Flow : My Levitical Poetic Doxology
By Aurora A. Ambrose/Vicki Evans

Psalm 91 Safety in God's Presence

Amplified Bible (AMP) https://www.biblegateway.com

¹ He who [a]dwells in the secret place of the Most High shall remain stable and fixed under the shadow of the Almighty [Whose power no foe can withstand].

² I will say of the Lord, He is my Refuge and my Fortress, my God; on Him I lean and rely, and in Him I [confidently] trust!

³ For [then] He will deliver you from the snare of the fowler and from the deadly pestilence.

⁴ [Then] He will cover you with His pinions, and under His wings shall you trust and find refuge; His truth and His faithfulness are a shield and a buckler.

⁵ You shall not be afraid of the terror of the night, nor of the arrow (the evil plots and slanders of the wicked) that flies by day,

⁶ Nor of the pestilence that stalks in darkness, nor of the destruction and sudden death that surprise and lay waste at noonday.

⁷ A thousand may fall at your side, and ten thousand at your right hand, but it shall not come near you.

⁸ Only a spectator shall you be [yourself inaccessible in the secret place of the Most High] as you witness the reward of the wicked.

⁹ Because you have made the Lord your refuge, and the Most High your dwelling place,

¹⁰ There shall no evil befall you, nor any plague or calamity come near your tent.

¹¹ For He will give His angels [especial] charge over you to accompany and defend and preserve you in all your ways [of obedience and service].

¹² They shall bear you up on their hands, lest you dash your foot against a stone.

¹³ You shall tread upon the lion and adder; the young lion and the serpent shall you trample underfoot.

¹⁴ Because he has set his love upon Me, therefore will I deliver him; I will set him on high, because he knows and understands My name [has a personal knowledge of My mercy, love, and kindness—trusts and relies on Me, knowing I will never forsake him, no, never].

¹⁵ He shall call upon Me, and I will answer him; I will be with him in trouble, I will deliver him and honor him.

¹⁶ With long life will I satisfy him and show him My salvation.

Footnotes:

a. [Psalm 91:1](#) The rich promises of this whole chapter are dependent upon one's meeting exactly the conditions of these first two verses (see Exod. 15:26).

"The Battle is The Lord's"

Yolanda Adams

[Speaking:]
What are you trying to say, Yolanda?
Look, forget about all that other junk.
This battle ain't yours, it's The Lord's.
Think about it and then start shouting, help me sing.

[verse 1:]
There is no pain, Jesus can't feel.
There is no hurt, that He can't heal,
For all things work, yes they do,
According to The Master's purpose
and His holy will.

No matter what, you in the balcony,
are going through, remember that God only wants a chance to use you
for the battle is not yours, it's The Lord's
We're gonna tell the devil that, all right?

There's no sadness, Jesus can't feel
and there is no sorrow,
that The Master is not able and willing to heal.
Remember that all things work,
they're not gonna be all good,
but they're gonna work according to God's purpose and His holy will.
No matter what, no matter what you're going through,
remember God sees all and he knows all
and all He wants to do is use you
for this Battle is not yours its, it's, it's, it's, it's The Lord's.

This battle is The Lord's. its The Lord's
(yes its the Lord's) it is The Lord's
(but in faith you've got to hold your head up high) hold your head up high
(you belong to the Most High God, you don't need to cry)
don't you cry, it's The Lord's
(its the Lord's) it's The Lord's
(yeah yeah yes its The Lord's) it is The Lord's
(No matter what) No matter what
(You're going through) through
(Remember it's gonna be alright, He's just using you)
God is only using you for He's worthy
(No matter what) no matter what
(you happen to go through right now) through
(Remember this will be a memory God is only using you)
God is only using you, for he's worthy
(You've got to have faith) No matter what
(You've got to know in your heart) through
(That no matter what comes, no matter what goes
God loves ya) God is only using you
(He loves ya *[7x]*)) it's not yours
(And this battle is not yours) no
(He needs a chance to prove to your enemies that He is God)
It's the Lord's, it's the Lord's, not yours
(So what you've got to do is, hold on, hold on) it's not yours
(hold on, hold on) it's not yours
(don't give up *[4x]*) it's the Lord's not yours
(Step out on faith) it's not yours
(no, no) no

(I'm so glad that God sees it) it's not yours
(and He knows all) it's the Lord's battle, not yours
This battle is not yours, no, it belongs to The Lord.
Hallelujah! Yeah!

Hallelujah, I'm Free!

Hallelujah, I'm Free! In Tribute to My Friend, the late Demita Usher

-Vicki Evans aka Aurora A. Ambrose

Don't grieve for me, for now I'm free,
I'm following the path God laid for me.
Gleefully I took His hand when I heard His call,
I turned my back and left it all.
I could not, would not stay another day,
Not even to laugh, to love, to work, to play.
The tasks left undone must stay that way,
For I've found that blissful peace at the end of the day.
If my parting has left for you an empty void, please fill it with remembered joy.
A friendship shared, a laugh, a kiss, Ah, yes, these things too I will miss.
Do not be burdened with times of sorrow,
I wish for you the sunshine of tomorrow.
My Life's been full, I've savored so much,
Good friends, good times, a loved one's touch.
Fulfillment of dreams realized, how I thank God for such!

Yes, maybe my time seemed all too brief,
Still don't lengthen it with undue grief.
Lift up your heart and share with me,
God wanted me now, He has set me free.
Shout Hallelujah, for I am free!
Thank you Demita, for always "Living Sunny Side Up,"
and inspiring the publishing of my first book.   I will see you in heaven.

What Do You Do When God Says No?

When we pray, The Lord God may answer us with "Yes," "No," "Maybe," "Wait" or "Not Now." I am particularly grateful for His non-affirmative answers to my requests, for in hindsight, I see now how He guided through or away from some situations that simply were not in my best interest. Hallelujah! As I've often heard my elders say and as I've often shared with others, "He may not come when you want Him to, but He is always on time."

One of my favorite musicals is Gershwin's "Porgy and Bess" in which the slickster, Sporting Life, keeps making trouble for other characters in this moving story. I particularly recall him singing, "it ain't necessarily so" and those words come to my mind when I think about situations in life where I thought my prayers went unanswered, when actually Father God keeps on looking out for me, always with my best interest at heart.

Surely, you, precious reader, may have had a similar experience. Let's look at eleven reasons for unanswered or differently answered prayers.

1. Sin in our lives. Reflect, confess, pray and repent. In Psalm 66:18, the psalmist wrote, "If I had cherished sin in my heart, the LORD would not have listened." God is able to hear our prayers, for He is completely omniscient. He maintains His distance when we allow sin to be a wall between Him and us. Major disobedience sets us up for longterm unanswered prayer. As First Samuel 8:18 states, "When that day comes, you will cry out for relief from the king you have chosen, and the Lord will not answer you in that day." This shows that He responds to our choice of actions, for He gave us free will, or the right to choose. Indeed, our loving God is in control, for He only wants what is best for us. What a loving Father He is!

2. Our loving God cares so much for us that He will not say yes to our prayers when doing so would bring us harm that we cannot foresee. For example, in Theology of Prayer, B.M. Palmer tells of a woman who spent the summer away from her children, and she was anxious to get back to them. When the woman learned that all the

rooms on a certain steamer ship were taken, she wept bitterly. Since she could not get a passage on any other ship, she was detained for two weeks in New York City. However, her sorrow of being so greatly delayed was turned into abundant thanksgiving when, within a few days, she learned that the vessel that denied her passage was buried at the bottom of the Atlantic Ocean. She did not realize the "no" as a wonderful answer to her prayer until the whole story unfolded. Once again, our loving God is in control, protecting her from unseen harm and danger.

3. Another reason that our prayers are answered with a "No" is because our loving Father God has something far greater in prepared for us. In the Bible, Mary and Martha really wanted Jesus to heal their sick brother Lazarus. Instead, He had resurrection in mind to demonstrate the power of God and foreshadow the resurrection of Christ. We ask for health, but often sickness,suffering or something far less than wealth is the best way to produce holiness, faith, perseverance and maturity in us. Our loving God is in control, shaping us to become more like Him.

4. Unknowingly, we pray in contrast with the purposes of other believers. For example, there are two Christians on opposing teams, who are praying for their team to win the game. In another example, there are two Christians who are applying for the same job. Also, as a third example, suppose there are two Christians trying to get their child in the same preschool. In each case, there are prayers at cross purposes of another believer. God must say "No" to one and "Yes" to another. Indeed, our loving God is in control, for He wants what is best for us.

5. We pray for things where it is impossible to give a "Yes" answer as in the following scenarios:

6. We pray for the wrong person to be our girlfriend/boyfriend or spouse, not realizing they do not have our best interests at heart. God has someone better for us if we will just follow His lead.

7. We pray that a missing child be found alive when they have, unbeknownst to us, been murdered.

8. We pray for lost things that are not found as in this example:

A carpenter was building some crates in which to place the clothing his church was sending to a Chinese orphanage. On his way home, he reached into his shirt pocket to find his glasses, but they were gone. He remembered putting them there that morning, so he drove back to the church. His search proved fruitless. When he finally replayed his earlier actions in his mind, he suddenly realized what happened. The glasses had slipped out of his pocket unnoticed and had fallen into one of the crates, which he had nailed shut. Now his brand new glasses were heading for China! The Great Depression was at its height and this man had six children. He had spent twenty dollars for those glasses that very morning. "It's just not fair," he told God as he drove home in frustration. "I've been very faithful in giving of my time and money to do your work, and now this happens."

Several months later, the director of the orphanage was on furlough in the United States. He wanted to visit all the churches that supported him in China, so he came to speak one Sunday evening at this small church in Chicago. The carpenter and his family sat in their usual seats among the sparse congregation. The missionary began by thanking the people for their faithfulness in supporting the Chinese orphanage. "But most of all," he said, "I must thank you for the glasses you sent last year. You see, the Communists had just swept through the orphanage, destroying everything, including my glasses. I was desperate. "Even if I had the money, there was simply no way of replacing those glasses. Along with not being able to see well, I experienced headaches every day, so my coworkers and I were in much prayer about this. Then your crates arrived. When my staff removed the covers, they found a pair of glasses lying on top."

The missionary paused long enough to let his words sink in. Then, still gripped with the awesome wonder of it all, he finally continued. "Folks, when I tried on the glasses, it was as though they had been custom-made just for me! I really want to thank you for being a part of that." The people listened, happy for the miraculous glasses. But this missionary surely must have confused their church with another, they thought. There were no glasses on their list of items to be sent overseas. Oh, but sitting quietly in the back of the church, with tears streaming down his face, an ordinary carpenter realized that the Master Carpenter had chosen to use him in a magnificently extraordinary way. Yes, our loving God is truly in control.

9. We pray for things that are already determined, such as praying for the salvation of someone who is already deceased, or praying for the successful birth of a boy or girl who has already been conceived. Certainly, God's timing shows that, as a loving Father, God is in complete control.

10. We get discouraged in prayer by thinking God has given a "No" answer, when in fact He has said nothing at all. Let us realize that "Wait" is an answer. A delay is not a denial. God often delays His answer to cultivate patience and persistence, as He builds our faith. He may also employ a delay to bring our will around to conform to His own. Surely, our loving Father God is in control.

11. Realize that God's "No" is not a rejection. Instead, see it as a redirection. Does one close a door to open a window? Of course not! In fact, God's "No" to one thing is a "Yes" to another as in the example from Second Samuel 7, where God said "No" to David's desire to build a temple.

I asked God several times to give me a good boyfriend but God said "No" or "Not this one" to those requests so that He could say "Yes" in giving me the gift of my Honey, who has helped my growth tremendously. Abba or Father God said "No" to healing my mango-sized goiter and thyroid issues which made breathing, speaking, teaching and singing painful. He helped me retire earlier than I'd planned to prepare me for a successful double surgery with five months of necessary recovery. This resulted in my best health ever. So I realize that my life journey is unique, and not meant to look like anyone else's, while Father God works in every detail to write His story in my life, a testimony of His Powerful Presence. Our loving God is in complete control.

12. God's "No" is not a punishment, rather it is a preparation. Notice Romans 5:2a-5: "And we rejoice in the hope of the glory of God. Not only so, but we also rejoice in our sufferings, because we know that suffering produces perseverance; perseverance, character; and character, hope. And hope does not disappoint us, because God has poured out His love into our hearts by the Holy Spirit, whom He has given us."

God is preparing us to be the Bride of our Savior, Jesus Christ, Who is King of Kings and Lord of Lords. In order for us to reign with

Him, we must be made into a bride worthy of our position. This is why He develops within us perseverance, character, and hope as we trust Him in prayer and are processed through life's difficulties. We are fully equipped with the Armor of God through diligent Bible study, meditation on His Holy Word, Prayer and enduring spiritual warfare as overcomers in Christ, in preparation for holy bridehood. Once again, our loving Father God is in complete control for our benefit.

13. Did you know that God's "No" will sometimes bring greater glory to God, our heavenly Father?

Notice Joni Eareckson Tada, who is a Zondervan publishing representative, of whom is often said, "Joni is one of the successful Christian writers who has remained the same person after gaining fame."

Notice Focus on the Family, one of my favorite Christian radio programs, which shared that a pastor's voice or throat was completely healed while being recorded. The tape was aired on Focus and he has now written a book. Hallelujah, our loving God is in control!

14. Sometimes, God's "No" opens the door to an adventure with our Father God, such as with Elijah in 1 Kings 19. He prayed that he might die. He told God, "I have had enough, Lord. Take my life. I am no better than my ancestors." God said "No" because He had an exciting adventure planned for Elijah! Notice 2 Kings 2:11: "Suddenly a chariot of fire and horses of fire appeared and separated the two of them, and Elijah went up to heaven in a whirlwind. Elisha saw this and cried out. 'My father! My father! The chariots and horsemen of Israel!' And Elisha saw him no more." Wow! That is amazing! Again, our precious loving God is in control!

15. On 95.9FM, The Fish, I heard about someone who prayed that God would keep this person of faith off of a jury. However, Father God had an adventure planned for this special person of two weeks on a trial where they ended up addressing the plaintiff from the jury box, urging him to forgive the man who killed his son. Look at that. As always, our precious loving God is in control!

So be encouraged by these accounts as you remember the scripture of Romans 8:28, Amplified Bible, which says,

<u>8:28</u> *We are assured {and} know that [God being a partner in their labor] all things work together {and} are [fitting into a plan] for good to {and} for those who love God and are called according to [His] design {and} purpose.*

So sometimes when things seem to be falling apart, they may actually be falling into place!

So draw near to our loving Father God, with a thankful heart and He will draw near to you as you become aware that your cup is already overflowing with blessings. Daily Gratitude enables you to perceive Him more clearly and to rejoice in your Loving relationship with our Heavenly Father God. He says in His Word, "*Nothing can separate you from My loving Presence!*" That is the foundation of your security. Whenever you start to feel anxious, remind yourself that your security rests in God alone, and He is completely trustworthy.

Realize that you will never be in control of your life circumstances, but you can relax and trust in His faithfulness and beneficial control. Instead of striving for a predictable, safe lifestyle, seek to know God in greater depth and breadth, for He longs to make your life a glorious adventure, but you must stop clinging to your old ways and notions of self sufficiency. Know that He gave His only Son, Jesus Christ, to suffer, die and rise from the dead on our behalf, to give you and me eternal life, if only we will graciously accept His gift. He is always doing something great, something new and something improved within the lives of His dearly beloved ones. So awaken with a grateful anticipation of all that Father God has prepared for you!

See, I am doing a new thing! Now it springs up; do you not perceive it? I am making a way in the desert and streams in the wasteland.
Isaiah 43:19

For I am convinced that neither death nor life, neither angels nor demons, neither the present nor the future, nor any powers, neither height nor depth, nor anything else in all creation, will be able to separate us from the love of God that is in Christ Jesus our Lord.
Romans 8:38–39

When I am afraid, I will trust in you. In God, whose word I praise, in God I trust; I will not be afraid. What can mortal man do to me?
Psalm 56:3–4

...He leads me beside the still waters...

Be a Victor: Overcome Adversity

There are many times in life when the unexpected, the unthinkable or even the egregious occurs in a totally unprecedented way, catching you off guard. Instead of losing faith, stop, be still and pray, for it is written in Colossians 4:2, "Devote yourselves to prayer, being watchful and thankful." Every time something derails your plans, desires and intentions, use that as a reminder to communicate with the Lord. There are several benefits to this practice, which, in my opinion, should be part of one's daily regimen.

Talking with God blesses you and strengthens your relationship with Him. Also, when disappointments come, they will not drag you down. In fact, instead of dragging you down, those disappointments are transformed by the Lord for good to those who love Him and are called to serve His purpose. In your relationship with the Lord, this transformation removes the intended sting from the difficult circumstances, making it possible to be joyful even in the midst of adversity. With Him, there is peace beyond human understanding, which is one of the caveats or benefits of having a relationship with

Him through accepting the gift of salvation through the incredible sacrifice Jesus Christ made on our behalf.

Begin by practicing this discipline in all the little or large disappointments of daily life. Often, these minor setbacks attempt to draw you away from God's omnipresent presence. However, when you reframe the setbacks as opportunities, you will find that you gain far more than you have lost. It is only after much faith training that you can accept major losses in this positive way. Still, it is possible to gain the perspective of the apostle Paul, who wrote in Philippians 3:7-8: Compared to the surpassing greatness of knowing Jesus Christ, I consider everything I once treasured to be as insignificant as rubbish. In simpler language, my own prayer is:

More of You Lord, far less of me
Make me who I am meant to be
You are all I want, and all I need
Lord, You are my Everything.
Take it all, I surrender it all to You.
Be my King. Lord, now I choose
More of You and far less of me.
All to You I completely surrender
All to You, my Blessed Savior
I surrender it all to You.
-Aurora A. Ambrose

Here's the bottom line from my own experiences. For example, after almost two months of hard labor, my paycheck was not received on time. At first, my emotions went from disappointment to fury then to tearful exasperation, which was increasing my blood pressure. Finally, I sat down and became very quiet. In the stillness, I prayed, read the Word and listened to wise counsel, as well as music that ministered to my weary spirit. I went to sleep trusting God to work it out. The next day, when none of my calls were answered by a particular person, I made a call to a more reliable contact. I learned that an internal file error was made that caused an egregious delay in being paid since my bank returned the improperly noted deposit upon receipt. In meeting the key people to discuss the next steps, the fact was revealed that the department had indeed received my appropriately filed update document but somehow used the deleted bank account for the automatic deposit. I made the necessary correction by filing the correct required information again and asked the personnel to call me when my money finally arrived in their office so that I can be called for immediate retrieval. Through it all, I learned to communicate effectively, deal only with the facts, get the desired results, talk with the bank as well as the particular department, call creditors to reschedule payments, and do it all in a calm demeanor without having to go to the extremes of filing a legal claim. All the way there and en route home, I continued to praise God for His calming, peaceful Presence. Surely God will get the glory for the resulting testimony when all this is resolved. Not only was I paid correctly, but the funds went to the proper account. Look at how God works! Meanwhile, I will always *trust in the Lord with all my heart, and I will not lean on my own understanding. In all my ways, I will acknowledge Him and He will make my paths straight*, according to the promises of Proverbs 3:5-6.

So, whenever things seem to be going wrong, trust Father God. When your life feels increasingly out of control, thank Him. These are supernatural responses, and they can lift you above your circumstances. If you do what comes naturally in the face of difficulties, you may fall prey to negativism. Even a few complaints can set you on a path that is a downward spiral, by darkening your perspective and mind-set. With this attitude controlling you, complaints flow more and more readily from your mouth. Each one moves you steadily down the slippery spiral. The lower you go, the faster you slide; but it is still possible to apply brakes. Cry out to Father God in His Name! Affirm your trust in Him, regardless of how you feel. Thank Him for everything, though this seems unnatural, even irrational. Gradually you will begin to ascend, recovering your lost ground.

When you are back on ground level, you can face all of your circumstances from a humble perspective. If you choose supernatural responses this time, trusting and thanking Him, as you realize that He is working things out for your good, you'll experience His unfathomable Peace.

But I trust in your unfailing love; my heart rejoices in your salvation. Psalm 13:5

Always giving thanks to God the Father for everything, in the name of our Lord Jesus Christ. Ephesians 5:20

<u>So, expect to encounter adversity in your life.</u> Remember that we live in a fallen world. Stop trying to find a way to circumvent difficulties to make life easier. The key problem with an easy life is that it masks your need for the Lord. When people choose to become a Christian, God infuses His life into believers, and empowers them to live on a supernatural level with His power by depending on Him. This reminds me of Mary Byrne's 1905 uplifting hymn from a medieval Celtic poem that I learned in choir rehearsal, "Be Thou My Vision:"

Be Thou my Vision, O Lord of my heart
Naught be all else to me, save that Thou art
Thou my best Thought, by day or by night
Waking or sleeping, Thy Presence my Light

Be Thou my Wisdom and Thou my true Word
I ever with Thee and Thou with me, Lord
Thou my great Father, I Thy true son
Thou in me dwelling and I with Thee one

Be Thou my battle Shield, Sword for the fight
Be Thou my Dignity, Thou my Delight
Thou my soul's Shelter, Thou my High Tower
Raise Thou me heavenward, O Power of my power

Riches I heed not, nor man' empty praise
Thou mine inheritance, now and always
Thou and Thou only, first in my heart
High King of Heaven, my Treasure Thou art

High King of Heaven, my victory won
May I reach Heaven's joys, O bright Heaven's Son!
Heart of my own heart, whatever befall
Still be my Vision, O Ruler of all.
Dallan Forgaill, 8th Century; Irish to English translation,
Mary Byrne, 1905; versed by Eleanor Hull, 1912

So, realize confidently that NOTHING takes God by surprise. In order to have a testimony, which is an experience to share how God has brought you through a difficulty, one must have a test. After all, it is in the test that patience, strength, faith and perseverance are developed. God will not allow circumstances to overwhelm you as long as you look to Him. Just hang in there, trusting Him to bring you through. He will help you cope with whatever the moment or situation presents. Collaborating with God brings blessings that far outweigh all troubles. Remain aware of His Holy Presence for it contains joy that can endure all eventualities. Reflect on Psalm 23:1-4 NIV:

"The Lord is my Shepherd; I shall not want. He makes me to lie down in green pastures; He leads me beside the still waters. He restores my soul; He leads me in the paths of righteousness for His name's sake. Yes, though I walk through the valley of the shadow of death, I will fear no evil; for You are with me; Your rod and Your staff, they comfort me."

Notice the clarifications for this favorite passage from the Amplified Bible:

Psalm 23 Amplified Bible (AMP)

A Psalm of David.

¹ The Lord is my Shepherd [to feed, guide, and shield me], I shall not lack.

² He makes me lie down in [fresh, tender] green pastures; He leads me beside the still and restful waters.

³ He refreshes and restores my life (my self); He leads me in the paths of righteousness [uprightness and right standing with Him—not for my earning it, but] for His name's sake.

⁴ Yes, though I walk through the [deep, sunless] valley of the shadow of death, I will fear or dread no evil, for You are with me; Your rod [to protect] and Your staff [to guide], they comfort me.

⁵ You prepare a table before me in the presence of my enemies. You anoint my head with [a] oil; my [brimming] cup runs over.

⁶ Surely or only goodness, mercy, and unfailing love shall follow me all the days of my life, and through the length of my days the house of the Lord [and His presence] shall be my dwelling place.

Take courage in the words of Second Corinthians 4:16-17: "Therefore we do not lose heart. Though outwardly we are wasting away, yet inwardly we are being renewed day by day. For our light and momentary troubles are achieving for us an eternal glory that far outweighs them all."

Therefore, anticipate coming face to face with life's impossibilities, situations that are totally beyond your ability to handle them. The awareness of your inadequacy is precisely the perfect place to encounter God's glory and power at its utmost as you turn to Him for help, wisdom and guidance. When you see these armies of problems marching toward you, cry out to the Lord! Allow Him to fight for you and watch Him work on your behalf. That is what He is here for. You were never expected to do it all on your own. As the famed Allstate commercial says, "Put yourself in our hands." Rather, put yourself in Father God's hands.

Put yourself in God's capable hands as you rest in the shadow of His Almighty Presence. Be encouraged. Just remember the words of John Mason Neale, 1862, as noted in the following poem, and Psalm 91:1, "He who dwells in the shelter of the Most High will rest in the shadow of the Almighty."

Christian, do you struggle on the battleground,
'gainst the powers of darkness closing in around?
Christian, rise, take armor, soldier of the cross;
For the sake of Jesus count your gain but loss.

Christian, do you battle Satan' power within,
All his striving, luring, tempting you to sin?
Christian, do not tremble, do not be downcast;
Arm yourself for battle, watch and pray and fast.

Christian, do you wrestle those who taunt and claim,
"Why keep fast and vigil? Prayer is said in vain!"
Christian, answer boldly: "While I breathe I pray!"

Peace shall follow battle, night shall end in day.
- John Mason Neale, 1862

May comfort and encouragement strengthen you as I close this chapter with the words of Karolina W. Sandell-Berg's 1865 hymn:

Day by day and with each passing moment
Strength I find to meet my trials here
Trusting in my Father's wise bestowment
I've no cause for worry or for fear.
He Whose heart is kind beyond measure
Gives unto each day what He deems best
Lovingly its part of pain and pleasure
Mingling toil with peace and rest.
Every day, the Lord Himself is near me
With a special mercy for each hour
All my cares He fain would bear and cheer me
He Whose Name is Counselor and Power
The protection of His child and treasure
Is a charge that on Himself He laid
"As they day, they strength shall be in measure
This the pledge to me He made.
Help me then in every tribulation
So to trust Thy promises, O Lord
That I lose not faith's sweet consolation
Offered me within Thy holy Word
Help me Lord when toil and trouble meeting
Ever to take as from a Father's hand
One by one, the days, the moments fleeting
Till I reach the promised land.

Now from Psalm 121:1-8, be comforted: I lift up my eyes to the hills, where does my help come from? My help comes from the Lord, The Maker of heaven and earth. He will not let your foot slip: He who watches over you will not slumber; indeed, He who watches over Israel will neither slumber nor sleep. The Lord watches over you: the Lord is your shade at your right hand; the sun will not harm you bye day, nor the moon by night. The Lord will keep you from all harm; He will watch over your life; the Lord will watch over your coming and going both now and forevermore.

Therefore, no matter what, keep praising God for He has you safely in the palm of His hand.

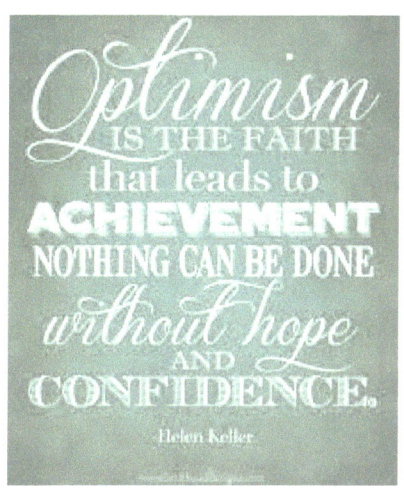

Be Optimistic

Let us take heed of the creed that formed my determination many years ago when I became a credentialed teacher and became an active member of 5-4 Optimist Club of Southern California, which inspired others to develop optimism as a philosophy of life, instill the value of volunteering in today's youth, develop citizens who have respect for the law, respect for themselves, and respect for the improvement of all communities. Now in the public domain, this creed was written by Christian Larson in 1912, and adopted in a shortened version by Optimist International in 1922. It has been a mainstay for many. It states:

The Optimist Creed

Promise Yourself

To be so strong that nothing can disturb your peace of mind.

To talk health, happiness and prosperity to every person you meet.

To make all your friends feel that there is something special in them.

To look at the sunny side of everything and make your optimism come true.

To think only of the best, to work only for the best, and to expect only the best.

To be just as enthusiastic about the success of others as you are about your own.

To forget the mistakes of the past and press on to the greater achievements of the future.

To wear a cheerful countenance at all times and give every living creature you meet a smile.

To give so much time to the improvement of yourself that you have no time to criticize others.

To be too large for worry, too noble for anger, too strong for fear, and too happy to permit the presence of trouble.

Enough said. Since the creed is self explanatory, do you know where the phrase "sunny side " comes from? Well, it was in 1899 that Ada J. Blenkhorn was inspired to write a Christian hymn, coined by a phrase that her young disabled nephew often used. Whenever he was being taken for a stroll outside, he always asked for his wheelchair to be pushed down "the sunny side" of the street. The lyrics can be found in the Cyber Hymnal, which specifies that these words are documented in the public domain. Since words frame our lives with substance and meaning, may these lyrics that Ada penned, upon which this book's theme is based, encourage, strengthen and uplift you.

There's a dark and a troubled side of life; There's a bright and a sunny side, too;

Tho' we meet with the darkness and strife, The sunny side we also may view.

Keep on the sunny side, always on the sunny side, Keep on the sunny side of life;

It will help us every day, it will brighten all the way,If we keep on the sunny side of life.

Tho' the storm in its fury break today, Crushing hopes that we cherished so dear,

Storm and cloud will in time pass away, The sun again will shine bright and clear.

Let us greet with a song of hope each day, Tho' the moments be cloudy or fair;

Let us trust in our Savior always, Who keepeth everyone in His care.

What does this song mean by the words "keep on the sunny side?" Here in the last four lines, noted in bold letters, the phrase means to anticipate each new day with a hopeful perspective, and live each day with faith and trust in God. The sunny side is determined by the words we say, the thoughts we think and our choice of actions. They are all related. As we think, so we are. Choose to be upbeat and positive, then watch the change in your mood, temperament and health.

Did you know that there is power in our words and thoughts? Yes, indeed. Whatever we say, we cause to happen by the energy we give it through the spoken word. What we choose, so it will be. Choose to speak life, joy, health and strength instead of speaking what is dark, dreary, anxious, full of complaints and negative. It is just that simple, yet that complex. Notice what is written in Philippians 4:4-7:

[4] Rejoice in the Lord always. I will say it again: Rejoice! [5] Let your gentleness be evident to all. The Lord is near. [6] Do not be anxious about anything, but in every situation, by prayer and petition, with thanksgiving, present your requests to God. [7] And the peace of God, which transcends all understanding, will guard your hearts and your minds in Christ Jesus.

This explains that unmitigated, incontainable joy should distinctively mark every believer in Jesus Christ. After all, as stated previously, Christian joy is not based on one's circumstances nor on religion. It is based on one's relationship with the Lord and the deep, abiding spiritual quality of life that comes from fellowship with Him, realizing how truly blessed one is. So rejoicing in the Lord is the key, no matter what may be, for He is with you, providing the grace, joy and strength to keep on keeping on.

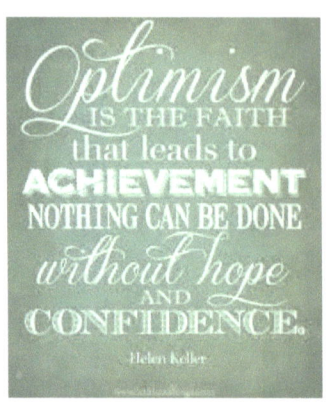

Moreover, this topic reminds me of the optimistic determination and dedication of the world's oldest female bodybuilder, Ernestine Shepherd. After listening to her interviews on YouTube, and with Dr. Mehmet Oz, I was shocked to learn that this vibrant, young lady I observed was actually 78 years of age! With the fitness and appearance of someone 50 years her junior, she related her love for people and her gratitude for her many blessings as she shared her motivation and strategies for achieving this Guinness Book of World Records accomplishment. In her interview on the Dr. Oz Show (Dr. Mehmet Oz, Television Talk Show, November 24, 2014, Channel 11 in Los Angeles, CA), Ernestine indicated that determination and discipline can make a difference in each of our lives as she encouraged and enlightened listeners by stating:

"My sister, Velvet, and I went shopping for bathing suits. When we saw how we looked in the mirror, we decided to do something about it. I was such a prissy woman. I didn't want to do any of that exercising. My sister was very active. When she started working out, she was 99 pounds and skin and bones. She had to gain enough weight to meet her goal of 140 pounds, which she did. I was 145 pounds so I had to come down in weight because I had all the cellulite, I had the fat in the back, and my legs were…Oh, my God… they were a mess. We were complete opposites."

"I made a promise to my sister that I would follow her dream, and it has become mine. She said that we wanted to inspire and motivate others to live a healthy, happy and fit lifestyle, to let them know that age is nothing but a number, and you can get fit. After my sister died from a brain aneurysm, I ended up with high blood pressure, panic attacks, high cholesterol, you name it, I had it. After a lot of prayer and help from my family, I could get on my feet again, and I started running. I found out I didn't need to take all that medication I was taking. My blood pressure went down, I stopped feeling unhappy, I stopped feeling depressed. People I know and people I don't know inspire me to keep going. They tell me how I'm helping them, and that was what my sister's and my dream was. So as long as I have breath in my body, that's what I want to do."

"When my sister and I began working out, she said, "We are going to be two of the oldest competitive bodybuilders." She said we were going to make the Guinness Book of World Records by the end as two sisters. Before she died she looked at me and said, "If I don't make it, you have to continue what we started. You have to make the Guinness Book of World Records, and you have to become a bodybuilder." I met the former Mr. Universe, Yohnnie Shambourger, and I asked him if he would work with me because I wanted to become a bodybuilder. I was 71 years of age when we started. He said, "You are going on a long journey, and you are going to have to follow everything I tell you to do. Do you think you can do it?" I shook my head and said yes. In a matter of seven months, he had me ready to be on the stage. We haven't looked back since then."

"Many times, people ask me what I do to stay healthy. This is my daily routine and what keeps me motivated to stay in shape, and I share this with the people in my workout classes."

"**2:30 a.m.** Wake up. Meditate and read devotions from the Bible. Eat a snack of a bagel with peanut butter and hard-boiled egg whites. Drink 16 oz. of water.

3:45 a.m. Head to nearby park and run 10 miles. Go home and eat breakfast of oatmeal, three hard-boiled egg whites and a tablespoon of walnuts. Drink 8 oz. of liquid egg whites.

8 a.m. Head to the gym and work out for 1 hour and 45 minutes.

10 to 11 a.m.: Train a group of senior men and women. The oldest woman is 89 years old.

11 a.m.: Train four to five women in the gym. Drink another 8-oz. glass of liquid egg whites.

1 p.m.: Go home and eat a can of tuna, a cup of spinach, ½ cup of sweet potato and drink an 8-oz. glass of water. REST.

6 to 7 p.m.: Teach another class at the gym. Head home and eat turkey, brown rice, broccoli, more egg whites and drink lots of water.

10 to 10:30 p.m.: Drink one more glass of liquid egg whites. Go to bed."

Now, despite all that Ernestine went through, this is proof positive that choosing to be joyfully optimistic and proactively getting into a better frame of mind can make an emphatic difference, not only in one's personal life, but also in the lives of those one encounters.

There is no need to be anxious, for that is counter productive not only to one's life but also to one's health. Often I hear people speaking only of the negatives in their lives. Listening to people during the typical day, I hear a litany of whining. Sometimes, I want to say to these people, "Get some cheese to go with your whine" but I'm sure they would not understand my message. If you dare to ask them how they are doing, usually a long laundry list of complaints comes pouring out, weighing you down the longer you listen. The more you try to encourage them, the more they complain about their situation, never once asking or caring about what is going on in your life. Instead, counting their blessings and proactively doing what can be done, getting the professional help that is needed to solve their expressed problems, is far more beneficial. For by faith, I believe that God is working on our behalf. So I refuse to be the enemy's prey, as I pray, speak, take positive action and keep on believing. All things are possible with God. This is how I stay on the sunny side.

The Benefits of Staying On the Sunny Side

Earlier I mentioned that the sunny side lifestyle affects our health positively. In a study mentioned by Danielle Dellorto (2014), it was determined that "happy people live longer and healthier lives" ("7 Ways to Boost Your Happiness," CNN, Danielle Dellorto, September 24, 2014).

Dellorto stated that Denmark has been ranked the happiest nation in the world. In a ten year Denmark study, researchers found that joyful, contented and enthusiastic people had a far lower occurrence of heart disease than those who felt happy less often. Since 1973, the United Nations and the European Commision have rated Denmark as number one in being the happiest nation. Danes have expressed that they are more satisfied with the general generosity among citizens, a strong support system and their freedom to make life choices. Additionally, Danes have a great work-life balance, meaning that they do not overwork... no workaholics are there. In fact, their average work week is only 33 hours and only 2% of Danes work more than 40 hours a week. In this study, researchers stated that Danes are more focussed on building memories, so they have a greater vitality and are closer to the people around them, which boosts their happiness. This difference is particularly noticed when compared with those who are focussed on material things, debt and the stress associated with keeping up with all those material things. Another factor discussed in this study is that Danes are social, and research shows that the more social people have a strong social support system, which lengthens telomeres (tiny caps on the DNA chromosomes that indicate cellular age). So, less friends can result in shorter telomeres and a shorter life. Moreover, Dellorto's article states that other studies show that loneliness leads higher rates of stress, depression and health problems. Therefore, it is recommended that each person have at least one close friend to boost on'e s level of happiness and health.

Additionally, Dellorto states that the Denmark study mentions that 43% of Danes regularly give back to their community as compared with 25% of Americans. Those who volunteer tend to be far happier with their lives and the joy of helping others starts early (Lara B. Aknin, J Kiley Hamlin, Elizabeth W. Dunn, "Giving Leads to Happiness in Young Children," June 14, 2012, Plos.org). It is more about performing acts of kindness, showing compassion, volunteering time and helping others by donating money, all of which increase happiness by improving one's sense of community, purpose and self image. Finally, the Denmark research states that laughter provides a significant boost to one's health. Did you know that when we laugh, our endorphins (brain and nervous system hormones) rise and our stress hormones decrease? These endorphins are the same brain chemicals that you get from exercise, associated with what is termed the "runner's high." Our hearts also benefit from laughter. According to a study, of the heart patients who were made to laugh daily, only 8% had a second heart attack within one year, while that was not the case with the 42% of non-laughers. There was no difference made in bodies between the results of real and fake laughter as the health boost showed similarly either way. As Steve Harvey often says, "Fake it until you make it." Try laughing a few minutes every day: find something funny, laugh in the shower, laugh at yourself, laugh at some funny stories, just laugh!

Also, when you shift from an anxious, hostile or depressed disposition to a sunny perspective, you fortify your immune system. In turn, this helps you avoid getting sick and even when you do get sick, you will have fewer symptoms. So a positive outlook truly makes a powerful difference in your health!

Dellorto also stated that studies prove that optimists have a lower risk of cardiovascular disease and overall fare better than pessimists (Harvard University, Harvard Men's Health Watch, May, 2008). Specifically noted in the findings were the following:

- People with positive emotions had lower blood pressure.

- Optimistic coronary bypass patients were only half as likely as pessimists to require re-hospitalization.

- Highly pessimistic men were three times more likely to develop hypertension.

- In one study, the most pessimistic men were more than twice as likely to develop heart disease compared with the most optimistic.

Upon viewing the results, scientists argued persuasively that optimism is good for health, given that healthy people are likely to have a brighter outlook on life that those who are ill. So to account for those who had per-existing medical conditions, the scientists adjusted their analyses and concluded from the studies that existing illnesses did not tarnish the benefits of optimism. One reason for this conclusion was stated as a behavioral possibility that optimists enjoy longer lives and better health because they lead healthier lifestyles, get better medical care and build stronger social support networks. Also, another reason is that optimism has biological benefits like less inflammation and lower levels of stress hormones. There is an additional factor mentioned in the Harvard study that states the possibility of genetic predisposition through heredity causing some people to be predisposed towards optimism, for which the same genes affect one's longevity and overall health. Finally, the Harvard study concluded that more study is needed to clarify distinctively the various mechanisms that are involved to bring this about.

Perhaps you remember the uplifting Bobby McFerrin song, Don't Worry, Be Happy. That popular title, "Don't Worry, Be Happy" is not just a catchy phrase. Did you know that a positive attitude can be a lifesaver, according to a recent study? In this study, researchers used a questionnaire to check the moods of 600 heart disease patients in a Denmark hospital, with a follow up five years later. They discovered that people with a positive attitude were 42 percent less likely to die during the study than those with a grumpier disposition. Also, those who were upbeat or exercised regularly were less likely to be hospitalized for a heart problem.

So no matter what comes during the day, good or bad, maintain positivity by doing the following:

- ❖ Eat good mood foods and eat at regular intervals throughout the day. By staying nutritionally fit, you keep your blood sugar stable, prevent anxiety and prevent mood swings.

- ❖ Get up, get moving! The more you exercise, the higher you boost your mood and protect your heart. Just twenty minutes a day combats the blues for twelve hours. Even if you sit at a desk most of the day, get up and walk at your breaks as I have done. Walking clears the mind and makes one feel energized.

This study is not the first to point out the link between being happy and being healthy. Researchers and doctors alike have long noted the direct correlation between emotional health and its effects on longevity. For example, people who are regularly pessimistic tend to suffer more chronic aches, fatigue and illness. In fact, negative emotions, like anger and sadness, also have a direct effect on brain function, increasing stress and our risk for heart disease, cancer and other serious diseases. Here is another optimistic example for all of us to follow.

Helen Steiner Rice, who lived from 1900-1981, was a beacon of comfort and inspiration through her prolific writings. One of her many poems is entitled, "Look On the Sunny Side," in which she emphasized optimism. Her life was characterized by her choice to be happy and value each day as a new day to say a kind word and do a good deed for everyone. She chose to use her talents to make others glad, not waste time nor energy by worrying needlessly. Her motto was to always look on the bright side of life and never be afraid of tomorrow, by realizing that we can rise above trouble and defeat. Rice believed that each day one should say that one is a child of God, and as such, nothing can harm one.

The B's of Joyful Living

We live in a world that is far too lacking in joy due to an overabundance of attitudes and lifestyles that bring people down, rather than lift them up. Here are some suggestions for restoring joy to someone's daily life.

Be just like an oyster.

Have you ever noticed how absolutely lovely a pearl is? This uniquely natural beauty is formed by a truly miraculous process that is completely unlike the mining process that is necessary for precious metals or gemstones which are both mined from the earth. In the development of a gemstone, it must be cut and polished to bring out its full beauty. Conversely, pearls do not require this type of a treatment. In order to reveal their loveliness, a pearl must be born completely from an oyster. Its iridescence, shimmering, soft and lustrous possesses a delightful inner glow that is unlike any other gem found on earth. Please be patient with me while I further explain the reasons I am suggesting that we all be just like an oyster.

Did you know that a natural pearl begins its life as a foreign object inside an oyster? Truly it does. A foreign object, like a piece of shell or a parasite accidentally lodges itself within the oyster's soft inner body, deep down inside where it cannot be expelled. Imagine something foreign and disagreeable getting inside your throat. Perhaps this has happened to you just as it happened to me. Actually, I remember a time or two when something went down my throat incorrectly and it was stuck there. I remember swallowing repeatedly on one occasion and it went down; on another occasion, coughing brought it out and I saw a tiny piece of food come out. Have you ever eaten something that disagreed with you? Well, I did and a process began inside me that provoked vomiting the remnants out of my mouth. Gross, but it helped me begin the process of feeling better. That said, imagine the oyster, doing what it does in the ocean, just minding its business. Along comes this object that enters the oyster while it is open, just planting itself there to make a home for itself. Just like something stuck in my throat or something unpleasant in my stomach, this foreign object does not feel good. In fact, it is creating an irritating disturbance inside the oyster. To ease this unpleasant irritant, the oyster's body, just like your body and even mine, starts to take defensive action. In fact, the oyster starts to protect itself by secreting a smooth, hard crystalline substance called a nacre all around that pesky irritant. That crystalline nacre is composed of microscopic crystals of calcium carbonate, each perfectly aligned with each other, in order that the light passing along the axis of one crystal is refracted and reflected by another, producing a glorious rainbow of color and light.

While this foreign irritant stays inside the oyster's body, the oyster will busily continue to secrete more layers of crystalline nacre coatings, layer upon layer upon layer. That irritant over a period of time will be totally encased by multiple layers of silkiness, created by the hard, smooth crystalline coatings, resulting in this uniquely gorgeous pearl. What an amazing wonder is this miraculous process where one of nature's most beautiful surprises is created just from the oyster protecting itself! Of course, there is a difference between natural and cultured pearls. Oysters will form a cultured pearl in the same way that a natural pearl is formed. However, instead of leaving the process to a chance occurrence, the difference is that a person will carefully implant an irritant inside the oyster, stepping back to let nature create its amazing miracle of lustrous beauty.

Just thinking about this process demonstrates how we are to be in our daily lives. There is a popular, anonymous adage that every day may not be good, but there is something good in every day. Romans 12:21 says do not be overcome by evil, but overcome evil with good. Certainly, just as I have, we all may have encountered someone in our personal or professional lives who seems stuck in negativity, as evidences by their daily comments, attitude and behavior. Unbeknownst to him or her, this person is an energy vampire, draining you of your optimism and joy if defensive action is not taken.

Like the oyster, you need to know how to deal with this for this person has been planted in your circle of influence. I have worked with people who are incessantly negative. I was working with one person who talked nonsense and negativity the entire time we were on the same assignment. Every time this person said something negative, I countered with something positive and proceeded to continue my theme until the person suddenly left. I breathed a sigh of relief and continued to listen on my ear buds to the spiritual nourishment that strengthens and sustains me. God's Word, traditional and contemporary gospel music, faith stories, inspirational podcasts, biographies of those who made it despite tough odds and good, clean humor are all instruments of rebuilding my faith and fortitude. For what is poured out of me, must be refilled in order for me to continue to be who I am designed to be.

Now this person was a tough assignment, for sure, but all believers are called to positively influence the world around us. It is our assignment to be a witness for Jesus Christ and be a positive reservoir of His light and love. Positive people, because of Christ being their center, have overcome their fears to such a degree that their beautiful energy flows outwardly. Consequently, they give energy instead of taking it, for in their presence, because of Who Christ is to them, you tend to feel energized, inspired, uplifted and ready to take on life's challenges rather than succumb to them. However, the Bible tells clearly tells us not to be overcome by evil, but we are to overcome evil with good. Sure, you may prefer to just exit stage left but what good is light if it will not change the darkness around it? What good is salt if it will not change the flavor of the food it placed upon? So, we know that this type of person has an endless capacity to dwell only on everything negative. Every time you see this person, they tend to complain, whine and moan about their lives, refusing to take responsibility for the results they see in their own lives. This person is full of fear, which blocks the natural flow of everything positive that is within him or her. Since they are choosing (yes, this is their conscious choice) to block their own positivity or inner light from God, they must get that light and positivity from others. Realize that just because a negative person has an endless supply of pity party invitations, "oh, woe is me," you do not have to choose to RSVP.

LOVE
bears all things,
believes all things,
hopes all things,
endures all things.

Reach Out

So, as oysters, let us consider how we can help a mildly or temporarily negative person who is drowning in a negative mindset. First of all, overcome darkness with light. Reach out with a kind word or gesture to cheer him or her up. Keep the conversation positive. Take him or her out to eat and talk about positive memories together. Sometimes just some positive attention is all that is needed to turn things around.

Throw Out

If this method is not successful, throw out the life line or the life preserver. Perhaps this person is much further out in the ocean of negativity. Maybe he or she is in denial of their problem even though everyone else can see it clearly. So, consider throwing out a life line or life preserver through a more indirect approach to help bolster their spirit. Give them a card or letter to show how much you care, or tell the person how much you care during a conversation. Use humor to break up the negative train of thought and bring him or her back to the shore of balance. One example of helping this type of person is to use an upbeat audio message or photo to insert into their electronic device. Send an inspirational message, YouTube video or song, as I have often done. I have even sent myself a song, link, photo or message, for it re-energizes me during my busy day. You see, everyone can benefit from a positive message.

It is just like when I was watching the television program, The Best of the Joy of Painting, where Bob Ross is demonstrating stroke by stroke how to paint lovely images. I watched one day as he painted a farmhouse scene, using dark hues to offset the lighter ones, creating a lovely softening effect much like an impressionist painter uses to develop the completed work. In the same way, the words we speak and the actions we choose can soften and sweeten the lives around us. After all, I have had my tough moments in life, and I am so grateful that someone chose to come alongside me each time and lend me a helping hand.

Row Out

Another great method to help a negative person is to row out to them with an intervention. Get several positive people together and visit the negative person. This gives more leverage than going alone would do, particularly if alcohol or drug influence is a factor in either the cause or the continuity of the negativity. Cast the light of awareness on what this person's words and actions are doing to worsen their situation. Offer all the combined help and resources that you can bring to the table. Help this person find their way out of the tunnel of darkness into the light. Extending the rowboat of hope, for there is always hope no matter how dark or foreboding things may appear to be. There is hopeful intervention in many organizations that help people through the roughest of situations: shelters like The Sheepfold for those who have been abused or endangered in some way, local churches that offer teaching and resources to mitigate difficult situations, ministries that help the homeless, organizations like food banks that feed the hungry and many more resources to help with every difficulty that people experience. Whatever is needed, seek out the help on the negative person's behalf. We are so fortunate to live in a world filled with free information right at our fingertips. Google, Bing, Ask.com and several other Internet search engines are available to research what is needed and render assistance in a timely manner, by pointing the way to where best that help can be found.

Go Out

As a last resort of assistance to someone who is struggling with negativity, try working one on one with the person to lift them up and bear them out of the incessantly negative mindset. However, just as in helping someone who is drowning, one must be careful remain positive so as not to be inundated and sucked down into their negative energy. Remember to keep yourself safe at all times with a gentle combination of genuine caring and detached awareness. You are the lifeguard. Do not allow yourself to be drowned by feeling so sorry for the person's sad story that you lose perspective on your purpose for being there. Stay positive, encouraging and upbeat. Above all, pray this person through their struggles. By seeking Divine help from the Lord, the Maker of heaven and earth, faith in His ability to turn things around for the best good can help, in addition to faith focused audio and written resources. All of these can enable one to choose love over fear, as we let go and let God help us overcome the most difficult of situations. One way that I help people is to quote song lyrics or a poem to uplift their spirits. One of my favorite songs that speaks to many hearts is written by Marvin Winans, who wrote:

"I've had some good days. I've had some hills to climb. I've had some weary days. I've had some sleepless nights but when I look around and I think things over, all of my good days outweigh my bad days, so I won't complain. Sometimes the clouds hang low. I can hardly see the road and then I ask the question, 'Lord, why so much pain?' But He knows what's best for me, although my weary eyes can't see, so I'll just say, 'Thank You Lord, I won't complain. God's been so good to me. The Lord has been so good to me, more than this old world or you could ever be. The Lord has been so good to me and He dried my tears away and He turned all my midnights into days. So I'll say, 'Thank You Lord. 'Thank You Lord. 'Thank You Lord.' I won't complain."

Be Joyful

Certainly, it is not always easy to be joyful at all times in our lives. Still, with the right perspective and a grateful heart, we can try to change our attitude. Although loneliness, sorrow, suffering and pain are a part of life, we can choose to look up and thank God for the lives we live, or we can choose to become bitter and focused on the suffering, forgetting that life on earth is only for a second, but eternity and where we spend it is forever. The second fruit of the Holy Spirit is joy, a concept which is further explained in the next chapter, entitled "Be Fruitful." Speaking to His disciples, Christ said in John 15:11, *"These things have I spoken unto you, that My joy might remain in you, and that your joy might be full."* In the Greek language, this word "joy" is translated as chara, which means cheerfulness, calm delight, and gladness.

Healthier and Happier for the First Time Ever

Having a joyful outlook is helping me achieve my lifelong dreams and inspire others to do the same. At work, in my daily activities and at the parks where I often exercise reflectively, there is such a joyful connection with others who share their stories with me as we encourage each other along the way. Since my thyroidectomy and goiter removal surgery, I gained back much of the weight I had just worked so hard to lose prior to my operation, recovery, due to the inability to move fluidly during recovery, attacked by constant excruciating pain. My head had to be kept upright in order for the stitches to heal properly. Talking was not allowed. Even the usual body movements had to be restricted, and every movement caused a deeper aching, which was helped greatly by the pain medication. Yet I remained grateful, so thankful to be alive and able to function more and more as each day of the four month recovery period passed. Although homebound, in the lovely stillness, I read and listened to encouragement, observed nature and wildlife, listened to hymns, gospel music and upbeat messages, many of which brought tears of abundant gratitude to my eyes. I particularly enjoy Bill and Gloria Gaither's program, "Precious Memories," full of inspirational songs and shared life stories. So many cards, calls and letters spoke to my heart! Eventually, I was able to type on my laptop to stay in touch with friends and loved ones. Time seemed to move at a snail's pace, yet I rejoiced to be visited by dear friends and feel God's abiding loving care through those He planted around me, enabling me to bloom in appreciation, wisdom, and courage. As more time passed, I was given the green light to talk and move about more, yet driving was still impossible since I could not turn my neck fully without turning my whole body. You never realize just how much your functioning depends on the mobility of your neck until something like this happens. Oh, how grateful I am to be able to move my whole body now! Now I stretch like a cat before moving, turn on music to do a little dance, occasionally I skip instead of walk, and when I see a swing, I'm on it like white on rice, swinging and kicking my legs gleefully!

Upon returning to the parks, I was welcomed heartily by the lovely wildlife and fellow exercisers. I felt God's Presence all around me, cheering me on, step by step. I thoroughly enjoy breathing in and out the fresh, fragrant, unpolluted air and seeing so many fraternizing geese, pigeons, sparrows, finches, swans and a wide assortment of ducks along my path, as I recalled the words of the hymn, "Why should I feel discouraged, why should the shadows fall? Why should my heart be lonely and long for heaven and home, when Jesus is my portion. My constant friend is He. His eye is on the sparrow, and I know He watches me." Overall, this helped me get my drive back. I'm feeling stronger, able to walk three miles around the perimeter of the park. Sometimes I sing, although only for a short period of time as that becomes painful with increased duration. Yet this joy I have is uncontainable, inspiring me to push forward and motivate others to be energized with a zest for life and a more joy filled perspective.

This is why I entered a two minute jump rope contest in hot July of all times of the year, knowing fully well that I was exhausted and not exactly a spring chicken anymore. Ooh child, that seemed to be the longest eternity of time, and the more I jumped, the more my feet and knees were screaming at me, "Hey you, do you want me to get ugly with you? Now get off of me!"

Well, I had another ten seconds to go, when my energy level just gave out on me. So I stopped jumping, panting like a weary roadrunner. Still, I rejoice that I had the courage to do my best, motivate others, and smile anyhow. My intent was to be an example to those who may have wanted to try but didn't have the nerve. Most of all, I am grateful that I had the wisdom to stop jumping up and down on that hard concrete without any rubber mat for support so that I could still continue to enjoy life daily painlessly, without overexertion.

Now that I've improved my eating habits to hydrating often and consuming more proteins, vegetables and fruits, healthy home cooking and eating less junk food, I am healthier, more upbeat, more energetic and focused at work because, thanks to my workouts, I am less stressed by work and life's concerns for the first time in my life. My sleep has improved dramatically, which restores my energy. There is even less of a desire to eat the junk foods, since there is no longer the emotional eating that was used to forget about the concerns that plagued me during the toughest times of my life. Who knew that joyful optimism actually makes one happier and stronger, able to endure hardships and improve one's health? What a major improvement! Thank You, Lord!

Everything that we experience and every person we meet has a purpose and a lesson to teach and give us. Pray and choose to be Joyful today regardless of your circumstances, which are allowed to instruct and strengthen you, polishing you into the diamond you were divinely designed to become with God's help. He will encourage and help you as you trust in and depend on Him. God knows exactly what you are feeling and He wants to have a conversation and a deeper relationship with you. He will advise and help you, so never stop praying. I Thessalonians 5:15-16 states, *"Rejoice always, pray continually, give thanks in all circumstances for this is God's will for you in Christ Jesus."* Also, James 1:2-4 enlightens us further: *"Consider it pure joy, my brothers and sisters, whenever you face trials of many kinds, because you know that the testing of your faith produces perseverance. Let perseverance finish its work so that you may be mature and complete, not lacking anything."*

Earlier in this section, I mentioned the hymn "His Eye is On the Sparrow." This song is inspired by the words of Jesus in the Gospel of Matthew 6:26 and Matthew 10:29-31: *"Look at the birds of the air; they neither sow nor reap nor gather into barns, and yet your heavenly Father feeds them. Are you not of more value than they?"* -Matthew 6:26

"Are not two sparrows sold for a farthing? and one of them shall not fall on the ground without your Father. But the very hairs of your head are all numbered. Fear ye not therefore, ye are of more value than many sparrows."-Matthew 10:29-31 I was reading about Ethel Waters some years ago, from her autobiography, entitled by the name of this hymn. It was inspiring to learn the origin of the hymn, originally written in 1905 by two Caucasian songwriters, composer Charles H. Gabriel and lyricist Civilla D. Martin. Civilla had this to say when questioned about her

sources of inspiration for the words of this song. In addition to the above scriptures, she explained:

"Early in the spring of 1905, my husband and I were sojourning in Elmira, New York. We contracted a deep friendship for a couple by the name of Mr. and Mrs. Doolittle—true saints of God. Mrs. Doolittle had been bedridden for nigh twenty years. Her husband was an incurable cripple who had to propel himself to and from his business in a wheel chair. Despite their afflictions, they lived happy Christian lives, bringing inspiration and comfort to all who knew them. One day while we were visiting with the Doolittles, my husband commented on their bright hopefulness and asked them for the secret of it. Mrs. Doolittle's reply was simple: "His eye is on the sparrow, and I know He watches me." The beauty of this simple expression of boundless faith gripped the hearts and fired the imagination of Dr. Martin and me. The public domain hymn 'His Eye Is on the Sparrow' was the outcome of that experience.

The beauty of this expression of simple faith gripped my heart and that same evening I wrote the words for the song. The rest, as they say, is history. If you're discouraged, afraid of the future, or struggling with the problems of today, listen again to the words of this beautiful song: "Why should I feel discouraged? Why should the shadows come? Why should my heart feel lonely, and long for heaven and home? When Jesus is my portion, a constant friend is He. His eye is on the sparrow and I know He watches over me. His eye is on the sparrow; and I know He watches me. I sing because I'm happy. I sing because I'm free! His eye is on the sparrow; and I know He watches me. His eye is on the sparrow; and I know He watches me." –Civilla D. Martin

These lyrics cause me to realize the difference between joy and happiness. Joy comes from inside the heart, knowing that God loves and cares for us. This knowledge does not rely on feeling happy about whatever has happened. Get it? Happiness relies on something happening, yet joy springs from within and endures no matter what your circumstances are. Certainly, one can choose to be joyful despite life's trials and challenges as James 1:2-3 points out, *"For you know that when your faith is tested, your endurance has a chance to grow."* As I heard a Sunday School teacher share many years ago, "Dealing with the unbearable is the beginning of the curve in the road to joy." So choose to be joyful! Allow your unbearable moments to bring you closer to the experience of God's ever present joy in your heart, for as Psalm 126:3 shares, *"The Lord has done great things for us, and we are filled with joy."* Joy is a fruit of the Holy Spirit's presence in your life: *"But the fruit of the Spirit is love, **joy**, peace, longsuffering, gentleness, goodness, faith, meekness, temperance: against such there is no law...If we live in the Spirit, let us also walk in the Spirit,"* Galatians 5:22-23, 25.

Did you know that joy is our natural state of being? Babies enter the joyful state so easily because they are fully in the present moment, instead of living in the past or in the future. Belief in God, and choosing to accept His gift of salvation to guide your daily life, help us to understand and see things in a different way from what the world presents to us. *"Believe in God; believe that He is, and that He created all things, both in heaven and in earth; believe that He has all wisdom, and all power, both in heaven and in earth; believe that man doth not comprehend all the things which the Lord can comprehend."* - Seeing and living in a Godly way, causes us to be happy and joyful in a far deeper way which only the Gospel of Jesus Christ can bring into one's life. That said, such a person is empowered to live according to His divine purpose. When you live a life of purpose, your relationship with time changes dramatically. Unlike others, you are not looking for happiness in the future, by saying things like, "When Y happens, then I will be happy and I'll be right where I've always wanted to be." No, instead you will be grateful in the present moment, thanking God for where you are, what you have and how things are better right here, right now. Herein you are saying, in effect, "Nothing could be more perfect than this present moment." Realize that the present is a gift. Be thankful for the gift! Where there is joy, there is inner peace.

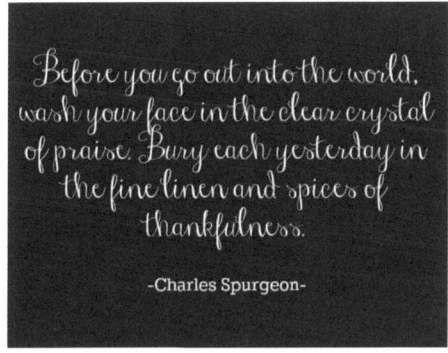

Before you go out into the world, wash your face in the clear crystal of praise. Bury each yesterday in the fine linen and spices of thankfulness.

-Charles Spurgeon-

So when you are faced with a decision, no matter how mundane it may be, choose what brings you closest to joy, for the joy of the Lord is the believer's strength, according to Nehemiah 8:10, and His Presence empowers you to be a victor rather than a victim, hopeful rather than one who suffers without hope. When you are joyful, life flows with lightness and ease, as you embrace with gratitude the life you live. God woke us up this morning, gave us a brand new day, filled with new mercies and opportunities. He led you to read this book, designed to uplift, encourage and strengthen you. Rejoice! Joyful feeling created joyful actions which produce more joyful feelings, so rejoice always, and again I say, rejoice! For in the words of Isaac Watts, penned in 1707:

"Come, we that love the Lord, and let our joys be known, join in a song with sweet accord, and thus surround the throne. Let those refuse to sing who never knew our God; but children of the heavenly King may speak their joys abroad. Then let our songs abound, and every tear be dry; we're marching through Emmanuel's ground to fairer worlds on high."

In this state of joy, empowered by Christ, we are enabled to stop worrying so much about our survival, as we trust in Him to help us. As for me, He gives me joy and makes my heart sing in praise. Through Him, we who are filled with His Spirit are enabled to be positive influencers of the world around us. Your focus will be on interacting daily without fear. People will be drawn to you like a magnet and your life will be filled with responsibly empowered relationships, to support others and be supported by others.

An Experiment

Many years ago, I taught a science lesson to my Sunday School class about overflowing joy as part of a unit on dealing with tough times in our lives. I used a 12 oz. clear drinking glass, a round cake pan; ½ cup of vinegar; one teaspoon of baking soda; one cup of water and five paper cups. I poured about 1/8 cup of water in three of the paper cups. I wrote the word "pray" on the side of one cup, "believe" on another paper cup and "Bible" on the third paper cup, and left the rest of the water for later use in this object lesson. Vinegar was poured in the fourth paper cup, where the words "Problems and Troubles" were written on the side of this paper cup. Baking soda was poured into the last paper cup and "Holy Spirit" was written on the side of that cup. Then I read to the class this passage of scripture in Philippians 4:4 which says, "Rejoice in the Lord always; again I will say, Rejoice."

God's Word tells us that we should always be joyful. This does not mean that we will always be happy, but we can still have joy, even when things aren't going well. When you trust in Jesus as your Savior His Spirit comes to live in you. The Holy Spirit produces fruit in your life as you listen to Him and you allow Him to control your thoughts, attitudes and actions. Joy is one of the fruits the Holy Spirit produces in your life. "But the fruit of the Spirit is love, joy, peace, patience, kindness, goodness, faithfulness, gentleness, self control…" according to Galatians 5:22-23 ESV.

When problems come into your life, Satan wants you to complain or worry and even doubt God; he wants to rob you of your joy. Remember, you have the Holy Spirit's power to win over Satan and be joyful even during hard times.

Today I have water, baking soda and vinegar. Now by mixing these three ingredients, something special happens that will help you remember to always have joy. Now this clear drinking glass represents your life. I will put the glass in the cake pan; (this is to catch the mixture when it overflows.) When you receive Jesus as your Savior, He comes to live inside of you by His Spirit. As I pour water into this glass, the water represents the fact that God's forgiveness washed away your sin and all of its punishment, so now you now have new life! (This is when I pour the water into the clear drinking glass until it is about half full.)

Next, the cup that has "Problems and Troubles" written on it is filled with vinegar. Did you know that vinegar is an acetic acid that is a weak acid which can be eaten. Eating this does not harm your body, but it does add a sour taste to your food. Just because you have received Jesus does not mean that you will no longer have problems. This vinegar reminds me of problems and troubles. Even though vinegar has a sour taste, it can add a good flavor to food. Well, God uses problems and troubles in our lives to teach us to depend on Him so that only He gets our praise. Now when problems come, you might feel like complaining, worrying, or doubting God. (This is when I pour the vinegar into the clear drinking glass.) But don't allow these bad attitudes and feelings to rob you of your joy! Instead, allow the Holy Spirit to produce the fruit of joy in your life.

Here's a cup of water that has "Pray" written on it. When problems come, one of the first things you can do is pray. Tell God how you feel and thank Him that He is with you as you go through this hard time. God tells us in Jeremiah 33:3, "Call to me and I will answer you, and will tell you great and hidden things that you have not known." (This is when I pour the water from the "Pray" cup into the clear drinking glass.) Next, trust or believe that God will help you go through this tough time. Here is another cup of water with the word "Believe" written on it. Jesus said in Matthew 21:22, "And whatever you ask in prayer, you will receive, if you have faith." Faith and trust mean we are to believe in God and have confidence that God will do what He says. (This is when I pour the water from the "Believe" cup into the clear drinking glass.) You have just talked to God. Now is the time that you need to allow Him to talk to you. Look at this cup that has "Bible" written on it. Spend time reading God's Word and allowing Him to speak to you. The Book of Psalms has a lot to say about praising God during our troubles. Listen to Psalm 56:2-4 which says, "my enemies trample on me all day long, for many attack me proudly. When I am afraid, I put my trust in you. In God, whose word I praise, in God I trust; I shall not be afraid. What can flesh do to me?" (This is the time that I pour the water from the "Bible" cup into the clear drinking glass.) So when you pray, believe and read the Bible. God's Spirit, living inside you will begin to change your thoughts and attitudes about the trouble or problem you are facing.

Here I have some baking soda in the cup that has the words "Holy Spirit" written on it. Now, watch what happens when I pour the baking soda into the water and vinegar mixture. (Now I pour the baking soda into the clear drinking glass. The liquid in the glass begins to bubble over.) This shows that when God's Spirit is controlling your thoughts and attitudes, then the fruit of joy will overflow in your life. When the vinegar mixes with the baking soda, the acetic acid in the vinegar neutralizes, or reduces the full effect of the baking soda. Then a gas called carbon dioxide forms. Carbon dioxide is actually the bubbles that overflow when vinegar reacts with the baking soda. This baking soda reminds me of the joy that comes from the Holy Spirit as you obey God and trust in His promises. The fruit of joy that comes from God's Spirit is a deep inner gladness you have because you know that God is in control. It's the inner gladness you have when you realize that God is faithful and always keeps His promises. Through His Spirit, God will give you His joy and strength to handle life's problems. In the Bible we read, "Do not grieve or be sad, for the joy of the Lord is your strength," according to Nehemiah 8:10. So, the next time you are facing a problem, please remember what happens when you add baking soda to vinegar. May each of you allow the fruit of joy to overflow in your life!

So choose to fulfill your mission in life, as God speaks to your heart, making decisions that strengthen your joy. In the words of the Twila Paris lyrics, "The Joy of the Lord will be my Strength; I will not falter, I will not faint; He is my Shepherd, I am not afraid; the Joy of the Lord is my Strength." Listen to the Scriptures that promise joy, and see why my heart is continuously so filled with joy:

*I will greatly **rejoice** in the Lord, my soul shall be **joyful** in my God; for He has clothed me with the garments of salvation, He has covered me with the robe of righteousness, as a bridegroom decks Himself with ornaments, and as a bride adorns herself with jewels. Isaiah 61:10*

*The Lord is my strength and my shield; my heart trusts in Him and He helps me. My heart leaps for **joy** and with my song I praise Him. The Lord is their strength, and He is the saving strength of His anointed. Psalm 28:7-8*

*For the **joy** of the Lord is your strength. Nehemiah 8:10b*

*I will bless the Lord at all times: His praise shall continually be in my mouth. My soul shall make her boast in the Lord: the humble shall hear and be **glad**. Psalm 34:1, 2*

*But let all those that put their trust in You **rejoice**: let them ever shout for **joy**, because You defend them: let them also that love Your Name be **joyful** in You. Psalm 5:11*

*You will show me the path of life: in Your presence is fullness of **joy**; at Your right hand, there are pleasures forevermore. Psalm 16:11*

*But You are **joy**, O You that inhabits the praises of Israel. Psalm 22:3*

*Weeping may endure for a night, but **joy** comes in the morning. Psalm 30:5*

*Your Words were found, and I did eat them; and Your Word was unto me the **joy** and **rejoicing** of my heart: for I am called by Your Name, O Lord God of Hosts. Jeremiah 15:16*

*But the fruit of the Spirit is love, **joy**, peace, longsuffering, gentleness, goodness, faith, meekness, temperance: against such there is no law…If we live in the Spirit, let us also walk in the Spirit. Galatians 5:22-23, 25*

***Rejoice** in the Lord always: and again I say, **Rejoice**. Philippians 4:4*

***Rejoice** evermore. I Thessalonians 5:16*

*My brethren, count it all **joy** when you fall into divers temptations. James 1:2*

*Let us be **glad** and **rejoice**, and give honor to Him: for the marriage of the Lamb is come, and His wife has made herself read. Revelations 19:7*

Let the words of Henry Van Dyke's 1907 hymn, composed to the music of Ludwig van Beethoven in 1824, from the 1905 Methodist Hymnal, speak to your heart when you need to be uplifted. In fact, the words were written by a great clergyman, poet and English literature educator of the 19th century who was a graduate of both Princeton University and Princeton Theological Seminary. Now Beethoven never wrote any hymns, however the music for this hymn comes from Beethoven's Ninth Symphony, since various people adapted portions of his music to serve as hymn tunes. Mr. Van Dyke was delighted by the joyful sound of Beethoven's Ninth. Therefore, he thought this should be used as a hymn tune, for he was well known for his devotional writings and seized by the visual beauty of the surrounding mountains while he was a guest preacher at Williams College in Massachusetts. That said, let the words of this inspirational hymn minister to you, for as I John 4:16 states, *"God is love, and those who abide in love abide in God, and God abides in them."*

Joyful, joyful, we adore Thee, God of glory, Lord of love;
hearts unfold like flowers before Thee, opening to the sun above.
Melt the clouds of sin and sadness, drive the dark of doubt away;
Giver of immortal gladness, fill us with the light of day!

All Thy works with joy surround Thee, earth and heaven reflect Thy rays, Stars and angels sin around Thee, Center of unbroken praise.
Field and forest, vale and mountain, flowery meadow, flashing sea,
Chanting bird and flowing fountain call us to rejoice in Thee.

Thou are giving and forgiving, ever blessing, ever blest,
Wellspring of the joy of living, ocean depth of happy rest!
Thou our Father, Christ our Brother, all who live in love are Thine;
Teach us how to love each other, lift us to the Joy Divine.

We each need to realize that life is a priceless gift from God. He designed us to live life to the fullest, or as one lyricist expressed, to "live life like it's golden." That means that we are to lead a life that is productive, rich and vibrant. Instead of looking for gray clouds in the sky, look for the silver lining in the clouds. Look for the best aspect of situations and people. Awaken to each new day with a song in your heart, ready to discover the rewards of living. This is what is meant by living optimistically, for in doing so, the optimist has a tendency to see the bigger picture rather than the minutia. As an optimist, I am driven by purposeful living, as evidenced by my checklist of aspirations, or as some call may call it, a vision board. After all, where there is no vision, there is no success in attaining one's goals. I appreciate the simple things in life. I have an immense respect for humanity as well as opportunities. For me, life is more about creating and treasuring memorable moments as I sojourn in this pilgrimage through life. To that end, here are some practical strategies to employ in your life in order that you may live more joyfully.

Silence and Stillness are Golden and Other Life Lessons

1. Silence and Stillness are Golden

We are surrounded by too much meaningless noise. However, we can turn down the volume on all the noise in our lives. In doing so, we will discover the amazing fact that silence and stillness are already here and have been here the whole time. When we daily and purposefully allow ourselves to be still, we naturally open up to a deeper appreciation of the present moment. We will become relaxed, more grounded and clearer. All of the stress will begin to melt away. What can you do today to bring silence into your life? When will you choose to just stop and be still?

2. Clean It Up Now

Recently I saw a television program that was dedicated to people whose homes and garages were filled with clutter. What a shame to observe such a tragedy because each person in that situation expressed their disgust, frustration, tendency to procrastinate and their resulting lack of joy. When I see clutter forming in my life, I schedule some time to get rid of it. I have several spring cleanings during the year to eliminate what is no longer needed, reorganize what is needed, and reflect on the best place to put it. Some of my wardrobe is in the garage to accommodate what is seasonal and necessary in my closet. If something is suddenly needed for whatever reason, I go shopping in the garage. What a treat! Also, it's very cost effective. Lately, I noticed that I had been out of touch with due to commitments, so I scheduled a get together with key people and started texting or emailing the rest as time permitted. As much as I like Facebook's ability to stay in touch with the wonderful people in my life, it requires more time than I have to keep up with the myriad comments that are posted, so I do that only as I am able. Next, I looked at how I am using the time and talents I am gifted with recently and realized that all work and no creativity is very dissatisfying. So I stopped making excuses and busily began to write as inspirations came to me.

So if there is any area in your life that you procrastinate about, pay attention and fix it. Find out what needs to be done to resolve the issue. Carve out the time, find the best solution, make yourself a committee of one and clean it up. This is how you make the space for joy and peace to illuminate your life.

> **Successful people never worry about what others are doing.**

my life.
my choices.
my mistakes.
my lessons.
not your business.

3. Mind your own business

The most frustrating unhappiness I've experienced came from and trying to control people and situations that I am unable to actually do anything positive about. It is what it is. I've learned to shut up, pray and move forward, for silence is golden. Lord knows my intentions were good though with more wisdom than I had at the time, things could have been done better. I've done the best I could, where and when I could, and with His help, I continue to live, grow and give for His utmost pleasure. As the quotes I saw somewhere said: 1) My life, my choices, my mistakes, my lessons, not your business; and 2), Successful people never worry about what others are doing. My mistakes have taught me volumes. Where I've erred, He has forgiven me, and I have forgiven myself as well as others. Enough said. The past is gone, so I cannot change that, yet I can learn from it and live better from those lessons. I realize that cannot change people unless they decide to be changed because they each have free will or the right to choose. However, I can do what I need to do to be the best me that I can be and do the most good. When I change, everything around me automatically changes. That is my sphere of influence where I choose to make the most difference with God's guidance. Now, look at yourself. If you are caught in a situation or in an emotional reaction, turn the mirror onto yourself to face your part in how it came about. Let go of the drama. Let go of your need to control and let God help you. See what is actually true and learn from your mistakes. Bring compassion where it is most needed. Diligently work on the areas where you get stuck. Then joy will shine through you.

> People that spend time looking for faults in others, should spend time correcting their own.

4. Give to Others

Our world is so focused on being needy for time, attention, love, and understanding. More, more, more is the outcry. When one lives in a state of lack, one tends to think that life only begins when one gets what is needed. Change your choice. Instead of living in lack, consider generosity. When you are giving, you are living by giving to others what you want or need. Pour yourself out by offering genuine attention, listening to others, showing interest, and caring for others' needs. You will become satisfied due to being transformed by sharing love with others.

5. Use All of Your Senses

This joyful, abundant life is right here for us to partake of, so slow down and be more observant, enjoying the moments as they come. Take the time to touch, see, hear, taste and smell the world around you, savoring it as you do. Even eating a peach becomes a sensual delight in this process, as you gratefully experience a symphony of enjoyment.

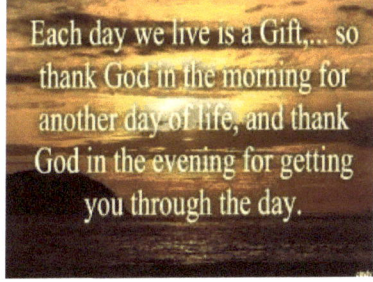

6. Take Stock of What is Working for You

It is too easy to focus on problems and feeling discontent. Stop allowing this negative energy to grab your attention. Negativity will not let go once you give in to it, for it is just as tenacious as a dog feasting on a juicy bone. I was driving to work one day, and just as I was about to cross the green light, I was delayed by a tiny dog in the middle of my lane. That little Chihuahua mixed breed was feasting on a meaty bone it had found right there in the street! The cars in front of me were honking at it yet I could not see what they were honking at until they had gone around it.

That's what negative energy is like, except it is gnawing on your mind, sapping your positive energy. So take charge. Take stock of what is working for good in your life. Do you enjoy your work? Is it your passion that you just love to get up and do? Is your living situation a good one? Do you know people who you love and appreciate? Do you enjoy your daily runs or a good home-cooked meal? Simply look around you and you may be surprised by the abundant bounty that is already present.

7. Love and Live, Be Willing to Forgive

Whether in love or just in life, issues do arise. When a grudge or difficulty interferes with your joy of life, then it requires your loving attention. Let not the issues or grudges multiply by the minutes ticking by. Let not your life be steeped regrets, doubts or self-righteousness. You be the bigger person if need be and start the process. Make amends sooner rather than later. When you feel wronged by someone or you hurt another, deal with it instead of letting it fester for when you forgive, you are set free to live joyfully. Neutralize the stories from the past, and make the choice to live joyfully now. You will be strengthened and empowered.

8. Learn from All of Life's Experiences

Sometimes the road of life is a bumpy one. If you want to master joyful living, be open to learning from life's challenges. Be honest about what pushes your buttons. Recognize when you have dropped into some quicksand that you can't seem to find your way out of. Difficult life experiences are designed to show us the areas in our lives where we are not yet free. Use these situations well for your own liberation, for the teachings keep coming until we finally understand the lesson. If you observe any self-defeating patterns in your life, slow things down so that you can become more aware of what you are doing and the catalysts that bring those reactions about. Choose to be proactive rather than reactive. Set the necessary boundaries in your life. Then you can make far better choices with your eyes wide open.

9. Be Pleasingly Pleasant

A pleasant perspective makes life more agreeable. No matter what is going on in your life, show up in an open, good-natured way. Choose to be positive and optimistic. No one likes a Negative Nancy. Stop complaining! Instead be patient, loving, open, kind, and agreeable, both in your daily life and in all interactions.

10. Decide to Drive in the Direction of Joy

Every moment offers a choice. Look at your life and your behavior to observe what you truly value. Are you choosing stress, conflict, and unhappiness, or peace, stillness and joy? Joy provides an excellent barometer for navigating through life. Recognize what brings you joy, then follow it. Make room in your life for what is full of light, optimism and purpose. This is the way to master the art of joyful living.

Be a Friend of Change

Change is inevitable. Nothing stays the same, so why not get prepared for change to happen? Be a participant in the change, and growth will follow. Refuse to change, and difficulties will follow, for you are blocking God's promotion to your next level of purpose.

Life seems easiest when you are young and unobligated to take care of any responsibilities. This is why it is essential that parents teach responsibilities to their children so that the discipline of taking care of a pet, doing certain chores or getting their homework done on time will already be well established in their thinking and lifestyle choices. Once you get older, trials and difficulties begin to shape your experiences and develop your wisdom. So choose wisely.

Failures and mistakes are the steppingstones to deeper growth. Learn the lessons from those mistakes and failures, and move on with your life.

Lessons learned:

> Wisdom is gained through experiences along the journey.

Things happen to guide you towards your destiny.

Blind trust in the Lord, following God's plan, causes time to fly by faster than you realize.

Don't lament about the past. Learn the lessons, do the work and grow.

Training is good but instinct is mandatory: one must know how to do what is required and why to do what is essential.

A lion raised in captivity knows nothing about how to live in the wild.

We each need to be with people who have our same rhythm; surround yourself with those who are likeminded in spirit, focus, perspective and vision.

Creativity seeks its own level. Don't apologize for being peculiarly different.

When it's time to leave the familiar to matriculate to your next level of growth, you must either leave on your own, or God will push you out, kicking and screaming. Which way do you often choose?

Nobody drifts toward discipline, wisdom, or humility. It is a daily pursuit.

Choose the values that bring you joy and are pleasing to God.

When I dare to be powerful, to use my strength in the service of my vision, then it becomes less and less important whether I am afraid.— Audre Lorde

Help and Joy in the Midst of the Storm

Lately, my life has been a series of storm experiences. There were times when I couldn't even think, because the pain I was enduring was so intense that all I could do was breathe. "Just put one foot in front of the other, and I will carry you," I heard The Lord say in my spirit. One death after another, three precious loved ones passed away within weeks of each other. My heart was hurting so badly that my tears poured out like rainstorms, in ebbs and flows. Whenever I least expected it, the least little word, fragrance, song or idea would cause me to sob profoundly all over again. There were other storms as well…struggles with time management, work schedules, finding peace and quiet in order to write, combating severe exhaustion, even struggling with emotional eating, just eating without a rhyme or reason, so emotionally drained from it all that I felt like I was sleepwalking through life. It helped to keep working, keep worshipping, keep praying, keep looking to The Lord. Through it all, my heart was aching yet somehow comforted simultaneously as The Holy Spirit ministered to me. My mind could not figure out what to do next, so The Lord showed me and even took the next step by step for me. Through it all, there was an unusual peace that I cannot explain as He guided me through the storms, putting my heart and mind, body and soul at peace as I continued to praise and worship My Rock, My Refuge, My Help. It is through this worship and praise of our Savior Jesus Christ that Satan, our enemy, and all his demonic minions must flee for they are overcome by The Light of The Lord, His Word, His Praise and His Worship. Speaking the Word of God over our lives and trusting Him as He keeps every one of His faithful promises strengthens us in the Faith. Father God's Truth prevails and prevents the evil one from deceiving our minds as we heed our Divine Shepherd's Voice. All fear, dismay, darkness and despair must retreat as His Voice of Truth and Salvation take hold, buoying us up over the waves of life's trials as we see firsthand the evidence that "this too shall pass" as He leads us beside still waters of rest and refreshment. Hallelujah for the testimony of faith and endurance, for yes, in Christ, we shall overcome victoriously!

Psalm 91, New Living Translation (NLT)

¹Those who live in the shelter of the Most High will find rest in the shadow of the Almighty. ²This I declare about the LORD: He alone is my refuge, my place of safety; He is my God, and I trust him.

Psalm 91, Amplified Bible (AMP)

¹He who [a]dwells in the secret place of the Most High shall remain stable and fixed under the shadow of the Almighty [Whose power no foe can withstand].

²I will say of the Lord, He is my Refuge and my Fortress, my God; on Him I lean and rely, and in Him I [confidently] trust!

Storms come to test our foundation of faith. Is our house of faith built upon the sinking sand or is it well established upon the Rock of Salvation, Jesus Christ? Do we really believe Him and His promises?

Surely, all storms or trials are an inevitable part of our spiritual life. The Bible says that it rains both on the just and the unjust. Jesus Himself gave a "weather alert bulletin" in the Book of Matthew when He said, *"Anyone who listens to my teaching and follows it is wise, like a person who builds a house on solid rock. Though the rain comes in torrents and the flood waters rise and the winds beat against that house, it won't collapse because it is built on bedrock. But anyone who hears My Teaching and doesn't obey it is foolish, like a person who builds a house on sand. When the rains and floods come and the winds beat against that house, it will collapse with a mighty crash."*

Matthew 7:24-27

Father God did a mighty work in me through this series of life storms. He was strengthening my faith. As I glorified Him through it all, He revealed His glory in the process. He used me to be a source of motivation, inspiration and encouragement to others, even while I was in the midst of all the pain. He caused me to write and speak His words before, during and after each funeral, and to this day, I still do not know what all I said. It does not matter. What matters is that lives were touched, hearts were moved and people were made stronger in the process. As The Lord God said in Exodus 33;19, *"I will make all My goodness pass before you, and I will proclaim the Name of The Lord before you. I will be gracious to whom I will be gracious, and I will have compassion on whom I will have compassion."*

Precious Lord, thank you, Yahweh, for preparing me for the bigger storms to come. I know this set of difficulties was a very small storm in comparison to whatever lies ahead. Thank You for loving me so much that You showed up when I needed You most, and You equipped me with what You deemed necessary in the moments of service, enabling others as well as me to grow closer to You. Thank You that Your Joy is my Strength. May my testimony lead others to true comfort and trust in You amidst all the storms that they are facing. May they be comforted and strengthened as You have been all this and more to me by this scripture:

"The Lord is my Rock, my Fortress, and my Savior; my God is my Rock, in whom I find protection. He is my Shield, the Power that saves me, and my Place of Safety." Psalm 18:2

In Jesus' matchless Name I pray, Amen.

Remember! Lost time can never be found.

Use the divine resource of time wisely.

God's Boxes

I have in my hands two boxes which God gave me to hold. He said, "Put all your sorrows in the black and all your joys in the gold. I heeded His words. In the two boxes, both my joys and sorrows I stored but though the gold box became heavier each day, the black box was as light as before. With curiosity, I opened the black box, I so wanted to find out why, and I saw, in the base of the box, a hole which my sorrows had fallen out by!

I showed the hole to God and mused aloud, "I wonder where my sorrows could be." He smiled a gentle smile at me, saying, "My child, they are all with me." I asked Him, "God, why give me the boxes: why the gold, and the black with the hole?" He replied, "My child, the gold is for you to count your blessings. The black is for you to let go."

Let go, and let God!

Be kinder than necessary, for everyone you meet is going through some kind of trial, disappointment, or struggle. Realize the blessing of friendship and treasure the joy each one is in your life.

Wine does not make you F A T .... It makes you LEAN ....

against tables, chairs, floors, walls and ugly people.

Think before you drink.

Be Wise with Your Greatest Power

Your greatest power is to choose, so choose wisely.

From the day we are born until the day we die, we each will make numerous choices that affect not only our own lives, but others' lives as well. Sometimes, those choices are made without thinking and taking the proper steps to make the wisest choice. A choice is a decision, a green light to move forward, a yellow light to pause, or a red light to stop altogether. When we make the best choices, we align ourselves to live the happiest life possible, just as a global positioning device uses longitude and latitude to determine one's location as accurately as possible.

This human journey called life typically follows a timeline during which many people tend to make the major life decisions within approximately the same periods of time. Yet the true adventure is learning who we truly are within by venturing into learning to value ourselves, our priorities and our unique gifts. Growth is a process, one to enjoy, although we don't always appreciate the difficulties while we are experiencing them. However, this life we live is certainly a mystery, filled with challenges to learn and own our personal truths, to grow in wisdom and knowledge, be of service to others, and choose that which will be the healthiest and most beneficial to us.

In my experience, as a retired veteran bilingual teacher with 30 years of service, specializing in educational technology, I have humbly learned that I do not know everything. Therefore I am a continual learner, striving to grow wiser and apply what I have learned to be of service to others.

By navigating through life's many experiences, I have learned a vast amount of wisdom either directly from both my own choices or vicariously from the choices others have made.

In my opinion, there is not enough wisdom being shared to enlighten people, for we each have been given a gift, a power, to choose. Sadly, many people choose poorly, not realizing until later in life that they could have done things better. To illustrate this, I saw a cartoon in which a single woman was given three wishes by a genie that appeared after she rubbed a magic lamp. She wished for wealth, then beauty and paused before making her final wish. The genie asks, "What is your final wish?" "Ah," she tells the genie, "For my final wish, turn my cat Bob into a handsome, loving husband." Poof! Bob the cat suddenly became a man. He stood before her, an athletic, muscular, handsome Adonis. She smiled as he embraced her tenderly, whispering gently in her ear, "Makes you wish you hadn't had me neutered, doesn't it?"

Here is a clear example of a choice that may not have been considered to be of personal impact prior to the three wishes being granted. Since life is a series of choices, or decisions which determine our degree of happiness, let us delve into the types of life decisions that shape our lives and the realities we create for ourselves in our interactions with others. That said, here are the major decisions that most people make during their lifetime.

Your health
How you think of yourself
Your values
Your attitude
Your life philosophy
Your aspirations

Your inspirations
How you handle life's many transitions
Your first job
How you handle relationships
Your choice to interact or remain aloof
How you handle issues at work
Your friends
How much money you save
How much you buy
Your education and/or continuing education
Your soulmate or spouse
How you raise your children
Your second career/changing jobs
Your retirement
Your level of involvement in community service

Something to consider
Vicki Evans/Aurora A. Ambrose

In the gardens of our lives
Where thoughts and ideas run wild
Weeds are ever trying to thrive
The slightest weakness lets them survive.

Be vigilant every day
As you go about your way
Guard what you hear, think and say
To live more Christlike in every way.

Choices that Impact the Quality of Daily Life

All of our choices make the difference, so choose wisely, for your greatest power is to choose. Many people think gardening is something you only do where there is dirt. However, realize that every day, we are tending our garden as planting seeds of ideas, mowing down weeds of unproductivity, tending our thought life which impacts our actions, leading others by example as a wise sage leads the novice gardener through useful tips and tricks of the trade to improve crops. In short, life is the garden and we are the gardeners whose choices make the difference between fertile harvests and dismal defeat. Herein lies the road we choose to travel. Choose wisely.

"Do not anticipate trouble, or worry about what may never happen. Keep in the sunlight." ~ Benjamin Franklin

Finally brethren, whatever is true, whatever is honorable, whatever is right, whatever is pure, whatever is lovely, whatever is of good repute, if there is any excellence and if anything worthy of praise, <u>dwell on these things.</u> Philippians 3:8

Be Careful to Reflect and Redirect

"May you live every day of your life."
Jonathan Swift

A few days ago I watched a news broadcast show a grieving family mourning the sudden loss of their teenage daughter. There was intense mourning, reflecting on her accomplishments in school and the warm memories shared by friends and family. It made me wonder how often we each re-evaluate our purpose as we move forward in life's journey. In the aftermath of such a tragedy, our thinking is reframed, maybe even totally overhauled with regards to how we approach our lives, our goals, and our relationships.

As I watched the broadcast I suddenly realized how the fragility of life makes every moment more meaningful. Many of us waste far too many moments immersing ourselves in needless distractions that steal our attention away from the things and the people that really matter.

If you feel like you're on the wrong track with what matters most to you, here are nine warning signs to look for, and tips to get you back on track:

1. You need to make all of life's decisions on your own. You are in the driver's seat of your life.

Some people seem to live their entire lives on the default setting, much like the settings that come with your new computer or electronic device, never realizing that they can customize everything. Each of us has a unique passion in our heart for something that makes us feel alive. It's each person's duty to find it and keep that passion fire lit. You've got to stop caring so much about what everyone else wants you to do, and start actually living for yourself with God's guidance.

1. Find your talents, your unique gifts and abilities, your strength, your love, your passions and embrace them. God created each person to be a unique vessel of autonomy, free will and choice. Determine what your goals and focus are. You are empowered to choose, design and experience your life. The life you create from doing something that moves you is far better than the life you get from sitting around wishing you were doing it. So get up and get after it.

2. Make your life choices confidently based on facts, doing your own research and accepting sound advice.

Never let your fear decide your future. To play it too safe is one of the riskiest choices you can make. Accept what is, let go of what was and have faith in what could be. The bold steps you take into the unknown won't be easy, but every step is worth it. There's no telling how many miles you will have to run while chasing a dream, but this chase is what gives meaning to life. Even if you have to fail several times before you succeed, your worst attempt will always be 100% better than the person who settles and never tries at all.

3. Choose the best possible path, not the easiest possible path.

Nothing in life is easy. Don't expect things to be given to you. Go out and achieve them. Good things come to those who work for them. Some have natural talent, while others make up for it with tremendous heart and determination, and it's almost always the latter group that succeeds in the long run.

There is too much emphasis on finding a 'quick fix' in today's society. For example taking diet pills to lose weight instead of exercising and eating well. No amount of magic fairy dust replaces diligent, focused, hard work.

Working and training for something is the opposite of hoping for it. If you believe in it with all your heart, then work for it with all your might. Great achievements must be earned. There is no elevator to success; you must take the stairs. So forget how you feel and <u>remember what you deserve</u>. NOW is always the best time to break out of your shell and show the world who you really are and what you're really made of. Start right where you are, use what you have, do what you can, and give it your best shot.

4. See the golden opportunities in the obstacles that you see.

The big difference between an obstacle and an opportunity is how you look at it. Look at the positives and don't dwell on the negatives. If you keep your head down, you'll miss life's goodness.

There's no shortage of problems waiting to be addressed. When you see problems piled on top of problems, and when there seems to be no end to the work that must be done in order to resolve them, what are you really seeing? You're looking at a mountain of opportunity. You're looking at a situation in which you can truly make a difference. You're looking at an environment where you can reach great heights by raising the stakes and pulling the reality of what's possible along with you.

When you look at an obstacle, but see opportunity instead, you become a powerful source that transforms grief into greatness.

5. Work smarter, not harder.

To achieve success and sustain happiness in life, you must focus your attention on the right things, in the right ways. Every growing human being (that means all of us) has resource constraints: limited time and energy. It is critical that you manage your resources effectively. You have to stay laser-focused on doing the RIGHT work, instead of doing a bunch of inconsequential work, right.

Not all work is created equal. Don't get caught up in odd jobs, even those that seem urgent, unless they are also important. Don't confuse being busy with being productive.

6. Finish the projects that you have started.

We are judged by what we finish, not what we start. Period.

Think about it, you rarely fail for the things you do. You fail for the things you don't do, the business you leave unfinished, and the things you make excuses about for the rest of your life.

In all walks of life, passion is what starts it and dedication is what finishes it.

7. Make time to connect with others in a meaningful way.

Never get so busy making a living that you forget to make a life for yourself. Never get so busy that you don't have time to be kind and connect with others. The happiest lives are connected to quality relationships. If you are too busy to share an occasional laugh with someone, you are too busy.

Truth be told, sometimes we're so busy watching out for what's just ahead of us that we don't take time to enjoy where we are and who we're with. So lift your head up today and appreciate those standing beside you. The people you take for granted today may turn out to be the only ones you need tomorrow.

Oh, and if you're currently on the fast track to success, be sure to be nice to people on your way up, because you might meet them again on your way back down. Remember life is a circle. Everything comes back around.

8. Concentrate your time on your support network because they make time for you.

Wrong things happen when you trust and worry about the wrong people. Don't make too much time for people who rarely make time for you, or who only make time for you when it's convenient for them. Know your worth. Know the difference between what you're getting from people and what you deserve.

Surround yourself with those who will support you whether it rains or shines. Above all, remember that people come and people go.

That's life. Stop holding on to those who have let go of you long ago.

9. Make a positive difference in others' lives.

Needless drama doesn't just walk into your life out of nowhere; you either create it, invite it or associate with those who bring it. Do not let anyone's ignorance, hatred, drama or negativity stop you from being the best person you can be.

Be an example of a pure existence. Don't spew hostile words at someone who spews them at you. Ignore their foolish antics and focus on kindness. Communicate and express yourself from a place of peace, from a place of love, with the best intentions. Use your voice for good: to inspire, to encourage, to educate, to pray, to counsel, and to spread compassionate empathy for others.

If someone insists on foisting their hostility and drama on you, simply ignore them and walk away. Sometimes people will talk about you when they envy the life you lead. Let them be. You affected their life; don't let them affect yours. Those who create their own drama deserve their own karma. Don't get sidetracked by people who are not on the right track.

Keep looking ahead to prepare for the next steps.

If you are reading this, smile. Although nothing in life is ever guaranteed, you can always choose to make the present a positive, productive experience.

What you do with this moment is what's most important, because the present is the steering wheel of your life. The only difference between where you are and where you want to be, at any point in time, is what you are presently doing. Your present actions can instantly steer you onto the right track. From this moment forward everything changes if you want it to. You simply have to decide what to do right now.

Take time to reflect on your choices and their impact.

In what way have you traveled down the wrong track in life? What have you learned and what changes have you made? What perceptions can you change to make this the best day ever?

The Best Day Ever: A Poem of Reflection

I just woke up and I realized…

This is the best day ever of my glorious life.

First of all, I am alive. What a gift, Lord, I give You a high five!

I didn't have to wake up. Could have been dead,

But God saw fit to give me life instead.

Got out of bed, grateful and glad that I'm moving my body

No pain, not feeling bad. Looked in the mirror, Wow!

Look at me! I am so thankful that I can see!

Opened my mouth, Said "Thank You Lord" for the ability to even

Say a single word. Looked all around me with a smile on my face

Just to have some food and not be hungry in this place.

Looked up above me and began to cry

For this roof over my head, I'm not on the street to die.

Looked in my pocket; How I rejoice!

There's some money in there! Help me make a wise choice.

Tears are flowing. Oh my, I can hear: Clock ticking, birds singing

With my open, working ears.

My heart is so happy to love and be loved

As evidenced daily by all these gifts from above.

So, if it is to be, it is up to me to do more good with positivity.

Peace and joy; Just so happy to be.

This is the best day ever full of opportunity!

Aurora A. Ambrose, Copyright AAA Productions

Start each day with joy and unending gratitude. No matter how easy it is to grumble, to shuffle groggily and to moan in complaint, instead choose to use that same energy to smile, rejoice, laugh and be grateful!

As my poem says, think of all that you can give thanks to God for: A brand new day of life. Air to breathe, the ability to make a difference, people who care about you, and so much more if you just think about it. Make it a habit to count your blessings instead of counting your sorrows. You are here. Life is a gift. What to you do with gifts? Whine and speak negatively? Of course not! Rejoice, show gratitude. You have a purpose, and a chance to make a difference in others' lives. So, get after it. Fun, grateful, positive, productive and healthy thoughts are not merely for children, you know, nor only for the rich, nor only for the happy go lucky. You need fun, joy, purpose, love and laughter just as much as you need air and food!

Maybe you feel that each day seems alike, dull, gray and grim. Maybe you are irritated by the little things, as you drag yourself to do one task after another. Maybe you isolate yourself from people for a variety of reasons, maybe you are thinking about all the wrongs that have been done to you, choosing not to "be so bothered with people." Maybe as you look in your mailbox, you then wonder why the invitations stop coming. Maybe you really aren't really sick but you're far from feeling well. Well, whatever the maybes are in your life, choose to stop and retool your thinking. For all you know, things are not as grim as they seem. Just the other day, I was driving to work. Things looked so fuzzy but it was a clear day. I thought to myself, "You need to clean this front window." So I did, but things didn't look any better. I leaned over to get my lint free towel out of the door's side pocket. My prescription Transition eyeglasses fell off. I picked them up and just as I started to put them back on, I saw all the dust that had gathered on them overnight. After cleaning them, I laughed at myself, thinking "Now that's a shame. Look at the difference now that I've cleaned my glasses!" So don't be so quick to judge the world around you. It may just be your perspective needs to be cleared like my eyeglasses. For when you change, everything around you changes.

Here's another thing to consider. Maybe you are always tired. Think about your daily schedule. Maybe you are a workaholic as I used to be before I learned to manage my time more strategically to balance my work with leisure. It is not always hard work that drains off your energy, but emotional disengagement as well as emotional upheaval are both unrecognized energy vampires. With those constant unguarded thoughts and negatively entrenched habits, your happiness and peacefulness are much more likely to become troubled. Choose to refocus your thoughts. For as a man (or woman) thinks, so is he (or she).

Keep your heart free from hate. Keep your mind free from worry. Live simply, expect little but give much. Fill your life with love. Scatter sunshine. Forget about yourself and think more often of others. Do as you would have it done unto you. For every day above ground, in my opinion, is the best day ever. Why?

The Best Day Ever Due to Seeing with New Eyes

Today, when I awoke, I suddenly realized that this is the best day of my life, ever! There were times when I wondered if I would make it to today; but I did! And because I did I'm going to celebrate!

Today, I'm going to celebrate what an unbelievable life I have: all of the relationships, the accomplishments, the many blessings, the opportunities, and yes, even the hardships because they have served to make me stronger and wiser.

I will go through this day with my head held high, with a happy heart. I will marvel at God's many amazing gifts: the morning dew, the sun, the clouds, the trees, the flowers, that butterfly passing by, the cat sitting on a post, the joyful gait of a puppy walking with its owner and even the rejoicing, ever singing birds. Today, none of these miraculous creations will escape my notice.

Today, I will share my excitement for life with other people. I'll make someone smile. I'll go out of my way to perform an unexpected act of kindness for someone I don't even know.

Today, I'll give a sincere compliment to someone who seems down. I'll tell a child how special he is, and I'll tell someone I love just how deeply I care for them and how much they mean to me.

Today is the day I quit worrying about what I don't have and start being grateful for all the wonderful things God has already given me. I'll remember that to worry is just a waste of time because my faith in God and his Divine Plan ensures everything will be just fine. Tonight, before I go to bed, I'll go outside and raise my eyes to the heavens. I will stand in awe at the beauty of the stars and the moon, and I will praise God for these magnificent treasures.

As the day ends and I lay my head down on my pillow, I will thank Him for the best day of my life. I will sleep the sleep of a contented child, excited with expectation because I know that just as today was the best day ever, tomorrow will be too, because my loving Heavenly Father is working everything out for good for me, just as He promised in Romans 8:28, due to my abundant love for Him, since He has called me for His purpose. Therefore, every day is going to be the best day ever!

May we never forget that this life is a gift. As my poem, "Best Day Ever" shares, "This is the best day ever of my glorious life." We each should realize the excitement for daily life we are to have. God has gifted us with the most wonderful present, Life. Rise up and give Him thanks for all the good He has done, is doing and will do. Every time we open our mouths, gratitude should flow out for every good thing comes from God's abundant provision. Stop bemoaning about life's obstacles. Don't you know that hidden within every obstacle is a golden opportunity? Each problem in life has within it an opportunity so powerful that it actually dwarfs the problem. After all, life's greatest success stories were created by people all throughout history who recognized at least one problem and turned it into a glorious opportunity! You could be the next success story. So let us worship Him and choose to enjoy this wondrous journey! Be happy for He is full of favor and honor.

"How lovely is Your dwelling place, O Lord of Hosts! My soul longs, indeed it faints, for the courts of the Lord, my heart and my flesh sing for joy to the living God. Even the sparrow finds a home, and the swallow a nest for herself, where she may lay her young, at Your altar, O Lord of Hosts, my King and my God.

Happy are those who live in Your house, ever singing Your praise. Happy are those whose strength is in You, in whose heart are the highways to Zion. As they go through the valley of Baca they make it a place of springs; the early rain also covers it with pools.

They go from strength to strength; the God of gods will be seen in Zion. O Lord of Hosts, hear my prayer; give ear, O God of Jacob! Behold our shield, O God; look on the face of your anointed. For a day in your courts in better than a thousand elsewhere. I would rather be a doorkeeper in the house of my God than live in the tents of wickedness. For the Lord God is a sun and shield; He bestows favor and honor. **No good thing does the Lord withhold from those who walk uprightly. O Lord of Hosts, happy is everyone who trusts in You."** –*Psalm 84*

O Lord, our Lord, how majestic is your name in all the earth! You have set your glory above the heavens. Psalm 8:1

Oh come, let us worship and bow down; let us kneel before the Lord, our Maker! Psalm 99:5

Worthy are You, our Lord and God, ro receive glory and honor and power, for You created all things, and by Your will they existed and were created. Revelation 4:11

Every good and perfect gift is from above, coming down from the Father of the heavenly lights, who does not change like shifting shadows. James 1:17

The Bee-Attitudes

Be led by the Holy Spirit. Now the Lord is the Spirit, and where the Spirit of the Lord is, there is liberty (emancipation from bondage, freedom). 2 Corinthians 3:17

Be free in Christ. And I will walk at liberty and at ease, for I have sought and inquired for (and desperately required) Your precepts. Psalm 119:45

Be uncomplicated. I am the Door; anyone who enters in through Me will be saved (will live). He will come in and he will go out (freely), and will find pasture. John 10:9

Be confident in God. Lean on, trust in, and be confident in the Lord with all your heart and mind and do not rely on your own insight or understanding. Proverbs 3:5

Be quick to forgive. Bear with each other and forgive whatever grievances you may have against one another. Forgive as the Lord forgave you. Colossians 3:13

Be honest. Do not lie to one another, seeing that you have put off the old self with its practices. Colossians 3:9; There are six things that the Lord hates, seven that are an abomination to Him: haughty eyes, a lying tongue, and hands that shed innocent blood, a heart that devises wicked plans, feet that make haste to run to evil, a false witness who breathes out lies, and one who sows discord among brothers. My son, keep your father's commandment, and forsake not your mother's teaching. Proverbs 6:16-20 ESV

Be outrageously blessed. Delight yourself also in the Lord, and He will give you the desires and secret petitions of your heart. Psalm 37:4

Through it all, may this book inspire you to live more joyfully, enjoy life and thrive by living a grateful life.

Life Lessons in the Aloha Wave

Since my excursion to the big island of Hawaii, I have often reflected on how liberating and serene life can be when the right choices are made. It never ceases to amaze me how surfers are able to bravely manage even the most dangerous waves ever seen, even as tall as ten to twenty feet in height. It seems that they glide through the waters effortlessly, yet I realize that, conversely, a great deal of effort is involved. After watching a few surfers, I overheard a buff surf instructor teaching a class, so I decided to take notes. Notice the parallels to our previous discussion on overcoming life's storms.

He shared that being in the right position to catch the wave is crucial to surfing safely just like having your feet in the right position is vital to riding a skateboard. Just as in life, it's all about keeping the balance. Are you stressed out and overwhelmed? Where are you in your life and life choices? Perhaps it's time to assess and redirect so that you can thrive instead of just surviving. Most surf spots get crowded, so knowing your place will lead to more waves for you. If you are too far off on the shoulder, you will get all the garbage waves. On the other hand, if you are at the center of the break where the wave peaks, and you don't know what you are doing, you probably won't make too many friends. It is important to know that there are two elements to what is called the 'line up.' The first line up is the actual position in the water, the second is the priority surfers give to one another so everyone gets a turn. Since there are not enough waves for everyone to enjoy, don't be a wave hog. Remember that taking your turn is part of showing courtesy to others. In life, it is irrelevant to be with the "in crowd"...particularly if they are not on the path or focus that you are trying to maintain in your spiritual, personal and business life. After all, birds of a feather flock together. Balance is what is vital, staying in step with The Lord, and in step with your purpose, while still enjoying having a life.

The line up in physical location means if you can keep your positioning consistent and make small adjustments to your location, then you will be more likely to find the break in the waves. To find your line, up use stationary and highly visible landmarks to position yourself with. Try to find two landmarks that are close to 90 degrees apart, one for your side-to-side movements and one for how far out you are. The currents and winds are continuous forces pushing the surfer out of position. Sometimes it is smart to stay with the group only if there are experienced surfers among them. If the waves are big, it's best to start your lineup outside or off to the shoulder, away from the break. This will allow you to get a feel for the current conditions and decide if it is even safe to be out there. In life, find the tried and true landmarks, people you trust, wise counsel and safe harbors where you thrive and grow best. Don't worry about what others are doing, you just stick to the path that God has for you. Whatever you do, give yourself a chance to take a break, make some highly valued friends, and learn to ride the waves with enjoyment. These and many other transformational lessons were learned in Hawaii that are fundamental to the transformations that now shape my life. May they inspire you also.

First, allow the Aloha Spirit to shape your day to day life. The Aloha state of mind is the embodiment of The Golden Rule, specifically, treat others the way you want to be treated, and love your neighbor as you love yourself. This means treating the world and everyone around you like they are a part of you. Living in the Aloha Wave incorporates sharing your kindness and wisdom, your heart, your talents and your true self with your community. No man is an island. Reach out and touch someone's life and in doing so, you are more enriched as you see how truly blessed you are, once you stop thinking about yourself and focus on others. When I was in Hawaii, I saw the natives come together to help each other out, cooking for one another, inviting each other over for a meal and laughter, teaching one another and visitors like me how to enjoy the island's beauty, sharing their life stories, cleaning up trash, walking, praying and talking together, repairing damage from a fire or storm, or patching up a home leveled by strong, rainy winds. Getting into the community and giving back is the cornerstone to Hawaiian life, and also to the Christian life. Giving rather than taking is the most rewarding way to be transformed, renewing your mind to rise to a higher calling of living. This can manifest as a smile, lending a helping hand or supporting a local business. What matters most is that everyone works together to spread the love, for where there is love, there is wealth.

Epilogue
Let Your Spirit Be Positive

Be joyful always; pray continually; give thanks in all circumstances, for this is God's will for you in Christ Jesus. - I Thessalonians 5:16-18

I Thessalonians 5:16-18 show us that every person is designed to live a joyful, prayerful and thankful life at all times. Having a joy-filled, cheerful heart is excellent medicine for us in addition to causing us to be a blessing to others, according to Proverbs 17:22, which says, *"A cheerful heart is good medicine…"* Through consistent prayer we are attuned to the Lord's purposes as He enables us to wait expectantly for His divine intervention. Having an attitude of gratitude continuously, no matter what happens, keeps our attention on our Almighty God, Who loves us limitlessly and is always faithful. It pleases Him when we have a lifestyle that inspires others and if fulfilling for us.

Finally, brothers, whatever is true, whatever is right, whatever is pure, whatever is lovely, whatever is admirable, if anything is excellent or praiseworthy, think about such things. Herein Philippians 2:8 encourages us to have a positive attitude by thinking about that which is admirable, noble, true or excellent. Since we live in an era that is conducive to doing wrong, let us be discerning and exercise wisdom in offering our respect and positive acceptance of those in authority.

Obey your leaders and submit to their authority. They keep watch over you as men who must give and account. Obey them so that their work will be a joy, not a burden, for that would be of no advantage to you. Hebrews 13:17

Let us be also be forgiving encouragers of each other, acting and reacting with the mind of Christ.

Do not be overcome by evil, but overcome evil with good. Romans 12:21

Bear with each other and forgive whatever grievances you may have against one another. Forgive as the Lord forgave you. And over all these virtues put on love, which binds them all together in perfect unity. Let the peace of Christ rule in your hearts, since as members of one body you were called to peace. And be thankful. Let the Word of Christ dwell in you richly. Colossians 3:13-16

It is vital to have a positive attitude toward our circumstances, for it is easy to be joyful and grateful when all is well. Yet we need to realize that it is not our circumstances that make us unhappy; actually, it is our negative attitude. Let us remember that suffering is inevitable, but misery is a choice.

With Christ, the Hope of Glory, walking beside us, living within us, praying for us, and holding our hands as we traverse through life's journey, we are inseparable from His love and intertwined intimately with Him. What an amazing, glorious wonder that surpasses all we can understand! When we quietly spend time communing and worshipping prayerfully in His presence, our awareness of His Life within us is heightened. Such knowledge is humbling and awesome beyond compare, producing within us the Joy of the Lord, which is our Strength. He fills us with Peace and Joy so that we may bubble over by the power of the Holy Spirit. Surely, through Him, our cup overflows. Remember:

More *Jesus*
Less Drama
Less Selfishness
Less Complaining
Less Bitterness
Less Gossip
Less Pride
Less Anger
Less Me

To them God has chosen to make known among the Gentiles the glorious riches of this mystery, which is Christ in you, the Hope of Glory. Colossians 1:27

Nehemiah said, "Go and enjoy choice food and sweet drinks, and send some to those who have nothing prepared. This day is sacred to our Lord. Do not grieve, for the Joy of the Lord is your strength. –Nehemiah 8:10

Remember also that we are called to trust in God. Sure, life often deals us an evil blow, yet we must remember that God is the One Who can turn this bad into good in the end. So cancel all pity parties, give God thanks and look expectantly towards the good solution He will bring about. This demonstrates our maturity as we trust in God, remain appreciative and stay positive, for He gives us strength. Be encouraged, be joyful and keep the faith.

In closing, may the following bless, strengthen and uplift you, enabling to do greater things to God's glory, as He has purposed you to do. Live joyfully!

May the God of your hope so fill you with all joy and peace in believing [through the experience of your faith] that by the power of the Holy Spirit, you may abound and be overflowing (bubbling over) with hope. – Romans 15:13 Amplified Bible

The Lord bless thee, and keep thee: The Lord make His face shine upon thee, and be gracious unto thee: The Lord lift up His countenance upon thee, and give thee peace. Numbers 6:24-26

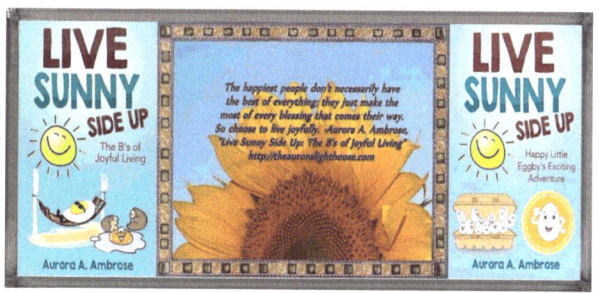

About the Author

http://theauroralighthouse.com/

Aurora A. Ambrose is a retired bilingual mentor educator, an author, and a bilingual substitute teacher. She has taught students of all ages for more than three decades, in addition to training new teachers. Aurora has a servant's heart. Her love for philanthropy, the arts, prose, lyrics, and poetry has inspired her to motivate and encourage others, just as she has chosen to do throughout her life. Aurora's writing experience includes, but is not limited to:

Live Sunny Side Up Book Trilogy: "The B's of Joyful Living;" "Green Pastures, Still Waters;" and the Children's Book, "Happy Little Eggby's Exciting Adventure"

Poetry Collections   Annual Journals for the non-profit, Los Angeles Music Week

<u>Songwriting, registered with BMI, Broadcast Music International:</u>

- ❖ As Soon As the Weather Breaks   Bobby Blue Bland
- ❖ Another Blues Day   Margie Evans
- ❖ Mistreated Woman   Margie Evans
- ❖ Can't Get You Off My Mind   Margie Evans

Album Liner Notes

❖ Too Late Rising Sun   Another Blues Day   We Shall Walk Through the Valley in Peace

Aurora's faith and interests provide her with opportunities to give service in ways that benefit the community. A continual learner and avid reader, she studies to study technology as well as varied methods of professional and personal growth. With a passion to help others, Aurora has a full and grateful heart, and desires to enrich others' lives by helping them see the silver lining of opportunity and purpose that are always present to develop our character through life's challenges.

About the Book,

Green Pastures, Still Waters: Overcoming in The Eye of the Storm

Green Pastures, Still Waters is the third book by Aurora A. Ambrose in the Live Sunny Side Up trilogy. Like

the previous two books, Green Pastures, Still Waters provides deeper insights, life lessons, encouragement and methods of dealing with life's various difficulties. Readers will be delighted by the whimsical stories and neighborly chats. There are also several passages that strengthen readers, providing strategic resources that enable us all to overcome life's toughest moments victoriously. Find your help and peace in the eye of life's storms as you learn to dance in the rain by reading "Green Pastures, Still Waters: Overcoming in the Eye of the Storm." Learn to see the silver lining of opportunity and purpose that are present in life's many faith developing and character building opportunities. Rejoice in your trials, for they are doors of opportunity.

www.ingramcontent.com/pod-product-compliance
Lightning Source LLC
Chambersburg PA
CBHW041429300426
44114CB00002B/15